Mindful

How to Lead a Happy Life and Rediscover a Healthy Relationship with Food or Drinking Get Rid of Emotional Eating and Find Peace Through Meditation

Written by Mark Goldstein

How Can You Lead a Happy Life and Build Healthy

Relation through Mindful Eating

Table Of Contents

Chapter 1

An Overview of Mindful Eating

I sit on the couch every day and watch TV with a large bowl of pastries or chips. I want to chew my light meals without thinking. In the middle of the TV show, I suddenly realized I had eaten it! Then I stood up and got more. Now I'm sure to taste every bite. - Rachel

Mindful Eating is the feeling of using your fingers to stitch each slice of potato, then taste salt when placed on your tongue. It is a matter of attention to hear the loud explosion of each mouth and hear the sound of chewing on the head. If you eat fried potatoes carefully, make sure they are consistent with the tongue and the pressure of the teeth. When chewing food falls, you will feel that your saliva is wetting potatoes and filling your neck. Understanding food means feeling the food in your stomach and feeling happy when you eat - or anything you feel. If you know, please pay attention to how to expand your stomach and feel full during meals. Everything feels from start to finish. They have slowed all aspects of food to fully understand the different parts and feel connected to them. This is just a small example of conscious food, and the book also includes many other foods. The basic message to keep in mind when reading is that changing the way you approach is not about identifying your domain, but about controlling your thoughts. You can do this by studying and understanding your mind, emotional mood and appetite, rather than controlling your usual old thoughts.

Mindful eating is a skill that can control your eating habits. It has been shown to promote weight loss, reduce excessive food consumption, and help you feel better.

Mindful food is not a diet. It uses a kind of meditation called mindful to help you identify and control your feelings and physical feelings. In this way, you can always learn about your experiences, desires and physical motivation.

Like most of us, you've probably eaten in the last few hours. Like many of us, do not remember everything you eat, let alone eat it. According to a report by the US Department of Agriculture in 2011, Americans are eating an average of two and a half hours a day, but more than half the time. Because we work, drive the car, read, watch TV or play with electronic devices, we do not know exactly what to eat. And this food is useless - lack of awareness of the food we eat - may lead to the spread of obesity and other health problems in the country, d. Lilian Cheung, nutritionist and Harvard School of Public Health School in Chen.

What is Mindful Food?

Food awareness is based on the concept of mindfulness and Buddhism. Mindful is a form of meditation that helps you identify and control your feelings and physical feelings. It is used to treat many diseases including eating disorders, depression, anxiety and various eating habits.

A healthy diet means attention, giving your food full attention and experience of your experience, desire and physical motivation. Mindfulness means that you are aware of the positive and encouraging choices to choose and prepare food, while respecting your inner wisdom.

It also involves all the senses of the diet, to meet your needs and to provide nutrition for your body. In addition to identifying food reactions (sympathy, disgust, or neutrality) without judgment, you will also realize the hunger and physical satiety that govern your decisions at the beginning and the end.

In short, mindfully eat include:

- Eat slowly, unhindered
- Listen to material hunger until it is full
- The difference between real hunger and non-hunger leads to food
- Treat your senses by sensing color, smell, sound, texture, and smell
- Learn how to deal with feelings of guilt and fear of eating

- Food that maintains public health and well-being
- Be aware of the effect of food on your feelings and your body
- I am very grateful for your food.
- With these things, you can replace your thoughts and answers with more informed and healthy answers.
- Mindful consumption depends on mindfulness, a form of meditation. Mindful eating means caring for your experience, your body direction, and your feelings about eating.
- I admit that there is no right or wrong way to eat
- Different awareness of the dining experience
- Accepting the dining experience is unique to everyone.
- Always pay attention to food
- Learn how to make decisions that promote health and well-being
- Pay attention to the relationship between land and biological and cultural practices and the impact of your choice.
- Promote balance, choice, wisdom and acceptance.

Steps to Mindful Eating:

The mindful means focusing on momentary moments, making recognition and accepting emotions, thoughts and physical feelings. "The principles of mindful also apply to healthy eating, but the concept of mind goes beyond individuals, including how to eat and how food affects the world," he said. Dr. Zhang. As of 2015, promoting the development of the American Nutrition Guide is the same concept, which for the first time includes the sustainability of food crops and the health benefits of food.

Although the ideal choice for a deliberate diet is similar to the Mediterranean diet, focusing on fruits, vegetables, whole grains, seeds, nuts and vegetable oils, this technique can be applied to burgers and cheeses. By paying special attention to the food you eat, you rarely enjoy this food. Eating mindfully means to take care of your food when you buy, prepare, serve and consume. However, practices that include some modifications may require you to deal with meals and snacks. If you want to avoid over-eating and gaining weight, controlling your blood sugar levels (for example, if you have diabetes), or just want to eat what your body needs, you will likely question this holiday goal.

But eating gently can help you. Mindful refers to exercise and they have a sense of time. This idea often occurs in the current place. Maybe we're studying what happened an hour ago, worrying about what will happen tomorrow, next week or worrying about what to do. Awakening encourages us to take note of these fears, and then gently back to the present.

Mindfulness can help you enjoy your food and enjoy full - moderation and self-control. Some studies suggest that mind training helps improve eating habits. A mindful diet can even help you lose weight if you eat too much or eat comfort or stress.

Here are some tips or steps to be more careful when eating. All these tips may not work for you. Try to figure out how it works.

1.Start Your Shopping List: Consider the health value of each item you add to the list and stick to any buying impulses while shopping. Fill most baskets in the product area to avoid crowded alleys of processed foods, potatoes and desserts.

2.Come to the Table with Your Appetite, but not when you feel hungry. If you miss a meal, you can put something in your stomach, so your first priority is to close the gap instead of eating.

3.Start With a Small Portion. It may be useful to set the panel size to 9 inches or less.

4.Enjoy Food. Take a break for a minute or two before you start eating, and think about everything you need to bring food to the table. In silence, thank you for the opportunity to enjoy the food and companions you love.

5.Bring all the Senses to the Food. When cooking, serving, and food, pay attention to color, texture, smell and even sound during cooking. When chewing, try to identify all ingredients, especially herbs.

6.Small Snacks. It is easier to taste food when the mouth is not full. Put your tools between pieces.

7.The Fabric is Very Good. The fabric is good so you can taste the essence of the food. (Based on what you need to chew it 20 to 40 times each time.) You'll be amazed at the taste of the version.

8.Eat Slowly. If you follow the suggestions above, please do not stop the food. Spend at least five minutes cooking before talking to your friends on your table.

9. Think

Take a moment to think about the feelings before you start eating. Are you busy or confirmation or sad or Bored or Hunger? What do you want, what do you need? Distinguish between the two. Once you think about the moment, you can choose to eat, eat and eat.

10. Turn off the TV (and all other offers)

Have you ever seen a mobile phone, tablet computer or computer asking where the food is? These disorders so we do not know what we eat and how much to eat.

11. Service your Part

Food is taken directly from the bag or box. If you cannot see how much you have, then it is not just easy to overeat, and when your food is not visible, it is hard to fully appreciate your food.

12. Expresses Gratitude

Before eating, taking a break, take a moment to appreciate the work done by your food, whether farmers, factory workers, animals, mother land, chef up your friends.

13. Chew 30 Times

Try 30 to make a thin candy from each bite. (30 is an approximate guide, because it is difficult to remove from oatmeal 10!) Before switching off, take the time to taste the mouth and texture. By letting the brain have time to send a message to say you've had enough, it can help avoid over- eating.

14. Leave the Club a Clean Plate

Training many of us who were doing everything on our plates even allowed us to leave the table to do it. You can terminate your membership in a clean dish club. Do not forget that the length of the packaging remains the way or allow the last bite. Even if no one likes to miss the food, we cannot help the poorest people.

Mindfulness Eating tips can Change Your Relationship with Food

Thank You:

Many of us have grown up in the family (or know someone has done it), and they pray or thank you before lunch.

But whether you do it yourself or not, you can refer to it and eat to express your gratitude.

Spend some time enjoying the food in front of you. Express your gratitude by thinking of assembling all the ingredients together to enjoy the important work of these delicious dishes (really, if you think about it, it's really cool).

This sport is not only good for your health but also helps you focus on your previous meal. This is the perfect workout to start each meal.

Eat a Little Slower:

There is the misconception that you need to do something slowly that makes you mindful.

This is not entirely true, but if you learn to practice mind, it may be necessary at first. The reason is that slow work helps us focus on spiritual activity.

The faster we go, the harder our thinking is to follow our bodies. Therefore, the delay is likely to be achieved.

Turn off the TV and Connect the Phone:

At this stage, this seems to be the first natural progression.

We focus our attention on the diet - including food and what happened at the time - so that all electronic devices can be used visually as attention to exercise.

Turn off the TV, turn the phone off, off, or at least keep away from the computer and anything else that might prevent you from eating.

Turn off the Tool:

It is located around the full presence of each bite.

As we eat often, we take a bite and prepare a new one once you chew it. This is a hidden copy of multitasking that is canceled through mind exercises.

When you just start practicing the mindful (or even exercise the mind), you will quickly notice that we do not know how to focus on the activity. Some multitasking tasks are extremely accurate and difficult to define. I began to exercise vigilance in change, albeit slowly.

The next time you eat, be careful not to miss the morsel in your mouth. Let your tools stand on the table and make them full of mindfulness.

Chew 30 Times:

How did the mindful eating change your relationship with food? I explained in five powerful ways how Buddhist monks and nuns chew at least 30 times each piece:

They do this to improve their awareness of consumption habits, with a focus on chewing, the center of mindful consumption.

Most of us eat, but we also just chew it a few times and then turn off the bigger pieces. We do not just eat fast, but we do not have much time to be present or rest. We do not know much about the digestive system.

By chewing at least 30 times at a time, we not only encourage practice, we have a more moderate body and mind.

While practicing this technique for the first time, it may be difficult to counter the desire to swallow food, but this practice will make it easier.

Eat Silently:

In addition to chewing 30 times each time they are chewed, you will enjoy the food more.

The reason is that the silence itself, and how slim it seems when we think about it, is actually feeding.

Explain why this is difficult, but any kind of activity, even simple conversation, will bring extra activity to your mind. If this activity continues, as always in our daily lives, it will continue to create more confusion and confusion (although it may be hidden).

It does not matter at the moment, but we need to take a break. It is easy for us to go back home, allowing us to do more. Therefore, it is an ideal complement to exercise the mind.

Take a Moment to Breathe:

You can stop eating from time to time and take some time to catch the weather.

You can pay attention to the quality of your breathing immediately, or deep breathe 3 times. If you are new to the exercise of the mind, I suggest you pay attention to your breathing.

This simple and effective mind exercise can help you focus on the essence, because the few minutes they often lead to futility and sleep (in the real sense).

Be a Food Critic

This is a tip from my favorite food on this list which will make you at a glance, so this is very helpful.

Be a critic of food (whether good or comfortable), eat slowly and carefully, and watch out for all the small flavors accompanying it. Pay attention to every feeling that every mouth can feel.

Of course, you cannot miss the terrible restaurant reviews. This does not help you much in your practice.

In fact, this is the only thing: this simple mentality is often enough to make the meal more thoughtful and deep.

Write Some Instructions:

During the meal, there will be some feelings such as hunger, satisfaction, fullness and sometimes fullness! Please pay special attention to these instructions.

In this way, you can easily observe other things that appear under full mindfulness, which increases your awareness and interest.

Turn the Fork:

This is a simple reminder to help you stay at the scene while eating. The idea seems simple. There are two ways to eat:

Tilt down - requires sharp movements, accuracy and attention. Laziness is usually impossible.

Everything says: Eating a fork and using a hammer to pick up food is the right way (at least most of the time) because it keeps you awake and there when you eat. It can help you eat well.

Change Your Utensil:

This is another simple and thoughtful suggestion, for the same reason, helps to change hands and reduce access.

You may have noticed that even if you can do everything mindfully, if we create the right environment, we can focus on our goal (in the case of a healthy diet), chewing, tasting, etc., so the mind will be greatly improved.)

The idea is simple: use another tool to make nutrition more difficult. This can be a lot of things, but the easiest and easiest option to get it is chopsticks and smaller spoons/forks.

Personally, chopsticks are always available, which really helps to improve my ability to exist while eating. They can be used to eat most things, so I recommend trying them out.

Of course, if you grow up in chopsticks, this may not be the case. Then think about it.

Eat Food That Needs Work:

Of course, you cannot always admire them, but if you can, you can have a meal or snack, all of which cost money. Such as grape seeds, pistachios or oranges.

This little effort to avoid seeds, cracking, peeling, peeling or orange peel can not only confuse food and create more species, but also helps you stay alert in a natural way.

Still need to eat more whole food, which is always good.

Drink Something:

As I said before, some activities are better in exercising the mind than others. Drinking is one of the activities. Especially things are too hot or cold.

You can have a regular cup of tea or coffee daily for breakfast or other meals. It is a very nutritious exercise, and it can make you wake up before eating. So this is a win-win situation.

You can read here how to do a simple meditation on Daydream (or Alternative Meditation).

Buddha Boiled

As I explained in this section and in the next section, a healthy diet can go beyond eating. To cook Buddha, you must pay attention to deepen the relationship with food and attention to mindfulness.

If you are cooking or preparing food while selecting, adjusting, chopping, and placing all ingredients (cooking utensils, pans, or frying pans), please pay attention to what you are doing now. You do not make food, you cook, and you do your full existence.

Why You Should Take Food Slowly:

The benefits of eating slow food include better digestion, better hydration, easier weight loss, ease of maintenance, and more satisfaction with our diet at the same time, indigestion for fast food, weight gain, and low satisfaction. The message is clear: reduce the diet and enjoy the benefits of improving health and well-being.

If you eat slowly, the better you eat. You are more likely to lose or lose. But they are also happy with every meal.

Conversely, when you eat hastily, the digestive system will be affected. The meal was very narrow. It seems that every meal is done very early, so you often want to eat more.

It's simple: reduce your diet and enjoy health and well-being.

The Value of the Slow Food:

We are a hasty, distracted and busy company. Most of North America eats fast. It is very fast that we rarely take the time to enjoy our food ... or sometimes even chew it properly.

No matter who we are, we will accelerate. Although you are a nutritionist, there are many other explanations for a master's degree in nutrition and nutrition. Like me

I want to increase in the next few years. Eating quickly helped me. I can get a lot of calories before my stomach realizes what's going on.

But now I get older, I just want to keep my weight. I must learn to eat slowly. This is not always easy. But if I did, thank my wife and my friends.

Although I recommend that my clients learn to eat more slowly, it is one of the easiest and most effective steps you can take to improve your overall health.

Why Eat Slowly?

Feel Good:

One of the main benefits of slow food is that your body has time to realize that you are full.

After 20 minutes of the meal, the brain sends a saturation signal. Most people do not have that much food!

Imagine the extra calories you can eat because you did not leave your body to realize that it no longer needs food. Now imagine the effect of these excess calories on your weight.

When we eat slowly, we also feel happy - not just "eat".

As you walk slowly, enjoy a meal, take care of your taste and touch, enjoy every bite, leave the table and feel your spirit ... even if you're just talking.

Improve Digestion:

Slow food also helps digestion.

Imagine digestion as a chain reaction. Once we see or grow up or think about food (step 1), we begin to put ourselves in the process of putting these foods in the mouth (step 2). Saliva contains enzymes that lead to deterioration of food and moisturize the mouth to enhance its intake.

At the same time, digestion stage 3, 4, 5 etc. should be ready to work. The stomach begins to secrete more acid. Our small intestine is ready to move.

As this process is accelerated, we force the digestive system to intervene before fully preparing. Christmas surprise is good, but digestion is not good.

At Rhode Island University, researchers studied the effects of early consumption levels by observing how 60 young people were treated.

- Eating slowly consumes 2 ounces
- It is easy to eat 2.5 grams of food a day.
- The consumption of fast food is 3.1 oz. Accurate. They also ate a bigger bite and chewed before swallowing.

This means that fast-food consumers will not only stop eating more food for a certain period of time, but will not be treated equally. In essence, the food will eventually become a great stomach to eat.

Digestion begins in the mouth, making it difficult to convert large, completely chewed entrees into partially digested food with mint, a mixture of hydrochloric acid, digestive enzymes and oral water. Remove the front gate valve.

Foods that are not properly distributed to the larvae can cause indigestion and other potential intestinal problems. Who wants it?

The Smallest Part - Do Not Try

Most studies have shown that slow food can help you eat less. This information is especially useful when trying to lose weight or avoid using it.

In another study at Rhode Island University, the researchers presented lunch or three regular lunches for 30 women. In either case, the flour consists of a large dish of pasta with tomato juice, vegetables, parmesan cheese and a glass of water.

At each visit, researchers asked women to eat comfortably enough. During the visit, they asked them to eat as soon as possible and during the second visit they were asked to eat slowly and put their cutlery between the bites.

When researchers compared the difference in food consumption between fast food and slow, they found:

In fast food, women are prohibited from using 646 calories in 9 minutes. By eating slowly, women consume 579 calories in 29 minutes.
Reduce 67 calories in 20 minutes!

If you conclude that they are three meals a day, you can see ... yes ... quickly ... you can defeat these extra calories.

There is an interesting change here: when women eat a quick lunch, they report hunger more than an hour after an informal lunch.

Food not only brings junk food consumption, but makes women unhappy! On the contrary, slow food naturally means less food, but satisfaction is more sustainable.

Improve the Hydration:

Proper hydration helps maintain fluid balance, activates muscles, makes our kidneys and intestines more effective, and improves skin appearance. The side effect of slow food is that it appears to increase the consumption of water during meals.

In fact, the same study at Rhode Island compared the number of water participants drank. When they ate slowly, the woman drank 409 ml of water. If they eat quickly, they drink only 289 ml of water!

These results make scientists sometimes wonder whether drinking more water can help people stay satisfied for a long time

Researchers at Rhode Island University tested this theory. (At the same time, you may have noticed that URIs is really worried about slow food consumption.) In a variety of lunch research, follow the water to allow participants to drink food. The amount of water is the same for each session.

Chapter 2

Lead a Happy and Healthy Life with Mindful Eating

Science Tells You That Mindful Eating Makes Your Day Happy:

Eat stress. This is something you do not do with divorce or feel lonelier than working. However, because four-fifths of people say they feel pressure at work, the office or business center can actually become a predictable place to work. Scientists have found that eating carefully can be an effective way to solve this problem and fight anxiety and depression. If you feel blue at work, food can be the biggest weapon of happiness, health and productivity.

What does Mindful Eating Mean?

Eating mindfully means knowing how to use, what to use, and why you are consuming this food. For example, cancer is focused on some external factors, such as:

- Size of the Portion
- Texture
- Temperature
- Food Color
- Number of bites
- Saturation / Obesity

- Percentage of micronutrients
- Where does the food come from?
- How food helps or nourishes the body

No one here is right or wrong. No manuscripts or mantras. All you have to do is be open when eating or having a snack, and be prepared to see something meaningful. You cannot do this if you try to perform multiple tasks at the same time and breathe for a few seconds while jumping or navigating between screens. You just have to be very distracted. Be prepared to stop juggling and eat alone.

Mindful Eating Reduces Food in a Refined Way:

Eating carefully will increase your chances of adequate consumption and getting into your body. By giving the body enough fuel, the energy and ability to cope with emotions increases. This allows you to communicate more or better with the team.

Taking care of food will make you feel the input of the senses. They tend to be more focused and accept emotions and facts. When this technology usually becomes, you can eventually move it to other areas. The idea of "putting 10 different things on me" can be said, "Everyone in my team has given this report something special." So stay agile and grateful.

Part of the mindful diet is the mindfulness of the past. For example, you might ask, "Can this food solve the fact that I will do it in the morning?" (Last), but you will also ask, "I have a creamy taste, is it really a disease?" (Current) "I was allowed to rest after lunch after the show ended" (Future). A less time perspective can lead to better decisions, help you avoid conflicts and achieve the goals you can be proud of.

If you eat your head, you do not have to avoid fast food altogether, but everything has a purpose, you know the purpose you choose. For example, you can cool ice cream pieces or chicken to return to your muscles. Therefore, the training asks an exact meal "why". This may be your day "Why should I pay attention to Opportunity X?" Or "Why does Sally feel nervous about his

project?" The ability to answer these questions will only help you identify people around you, but it will also make you feel like work is not important.

Eating will force you to slow down and think. In this way, you can prevent yourself from making quick decisions and regretting later. It can also help you maintain a broader perspective and make you more creative and respectful.

A Good Tool to Expand your Emotional Library:

Unlike other "treatments", a cautious diet is completely free and you and your staff can train every day. Combine them with other positive strategies - listen to music, decorate your room with personal items or take a short break in yoga - work suddenly improves.

Understanding the Mindful Eating and its Relation to Health:

Mindful is an art that simply observes and records what is happening now - no need to rely on or judge it. In traditional mind meditation, this can translate into observing your thoughts and feelings, with some disengaging as they appear and disappear. By being a witness to your heart and the thoughts flowing through it, you become an independent observer and can feel peace with the present.

When you apply your mind to your diet, you just need to take a look at all aspects of your consumption, so that a simple meal can be transformed into a rich experience. However, the gift offered by the mind diet is more than just a comfortable and enjoyable meal! By being keenly aware of and adapting to your dietary choices, a conscious diet can be a very quiet exercise with far-reaching benefits for physical, mental and emotional well-being, including:

1. **Reducing stress:** As a meditation method, attention to diet can stimulate the sympathetic nervous system and reduce response

2. **Improve mood:** A mind diet can help you improve your posture more peaceful and optimistic

3. **Maintain a healthy relationship with food:** Be careful when eating to reduce excessive eating or eating when you are not hungry

4. Best weight: Studies have shown that mind exercises such as the mind diet can help reduce body weight and reduce the accumulation of fat in the abdomen.

5. More effective digestion: Eat slowly, let your body make better use of nutrition and help you feel comfortable after a meal.

6. Blood sugar levels and healthy fats: After one year of study, people who have been carefully taken can reduce blood sugar levels and triglyceride levels.

7. Vibrant Germ Health: All other benefits of a vigilant diet create the conditions for budding intestinal friendly plants!

Mindful Eating Change Your Life:

Do you depend on sugar, processed foods, and unhealthy foods? Simplify feelings and stress in your life and give you more and more things you do not know to eat. Are you concerned that it is impossible to quit your addiction to sugar, soft drinks and fast food?

Fear, not because you acquired the taste of unhealthy food and lost everything. This does not mean that you have to fall into the temptations and desires of life and get a great weight. Your brain has the solution as always, and attention is the key to success.

Imagine learning a new way of thinking and eating so that you can fully experience and incorporate new flavors and textures into your food, not just eat and satisfy yourself without dissatisfaction immediately. A new way to eat well for your mood and good health.

Do you want to know how to change and learn to eat more carefully and interfere with your addiction to unhealthy foods?

What is the Secret of Success?

Remember to respect your body and understand the impact of your eating habits and lifestyle on your future, health and well-being until you get the best version of prosperity and life. I know from experience that I gained weight because I often tend to seduce, tolerate my feelings, and always drink them with unhealthy eating. I care a lot because my trust and inability to control these feelings makes me over-react to the situation in my life. Emotional diners have become meaningless. I have five stones, I am sick, I am in the sand until I get the last statement, I think I will change my decision.

You saw me three years later and accepted the gift. I believe that a happy and healthy life is real, and I can fully experience physical and mental growth and new energy in my life. I am from survival to prosperity.

Mindful eating not only changed my life but also saved my life. I am now eating my health and happiness, not increasing my comfort or hurting my feelings. I use my food as fuel instead of therapy.

By focusing on your diet and eating habits, you will hear better about your body and satisfaction. This helps you understand what your body and spirit tell you or what is confusing, and helps you determine when you feel hungry and how you can best support it. Think about it and tell yourself

"I appreciate my body, so I will see what I eat and what I want to eat."

Here are Some tips for Starting a Mindful Eating Trip towards Happy Life

1. Carry Food with You and Eat Without Intervention:

It does not seem easy to eat at first, but once you start, you'll find it difficult. However, this is an essential step in a careful diet and lifestyle change. In order to enjoy full food, sit down to eat, focus on the pleasure of eating, and appreciate the taste and taste it provides. No TV. No cell phone. Do not read. No laptop, just you, your food and all your attention.

2. Make Choices Every Day and Promise to Change:

Healthy eating will not be better than it is now. It's time to rejuvenate the life you want. I asked what you want in your life today. Let yourself be in charge of the future in the future. Stephen Koffie, author of Seven Habits for the Highly Qualified: "Responsibility gives a response." Let yourself assume responsibility and will respond both to body and mind.

3. Calm and Keep Your Body Relaxed:

In order to digest food and absorb nutrients, your body must relax.

We often multitask and travel.

When we activate the body's response to stress, we are in a state of extreme anxiety, laughing at everything that awaits us, and once again reflecting on what it contains or the benefits it brings to our health and our well-being.

When we eat in multitasking, we do not know hunger and inner richness, which helps us, determine when we are happy and can stop eating as much as possible. It is easy to eat too much after the meal and is always hungry.

If you have a desire to change and change the way you eat, discipline, motivation, and live the life you deserve, read more about the free path to change your conscious lifestyle.

"You have to eat to live, not to eat." - Benjamin Franklin

Mindful Eating Helps You to Become Healthier and More Fulfilled:

How our diet affects our health and well-being, as well as our diet. Have you ever seen the fun of a TV or computer, and suddenly did not realize that he used all the chip bags? Even if you eat more than you need, you may not feel good.

The first step in choosing healthy food is to learn more about our food.

There is a science behind it. After dinner, our intestines release the peptide that tells us that we are no longer hungry. If we eat very quickly, the process is not fast enough, so our minds know they are no longer eating. So, we still eat and eat a lot.

A more cautious approach to food allows our mother to follow a natural approach. Start by slowing down and gradually understanding the eating experience. This means that you focus all your attention on the eating process. Focus all your senses on food and try to understand your thoughts, feelings, and physical feelings. Even with a small deliberate bite, we can see an increase in smell and taste.

Studies have shown that food becomes smaller and more comfortable after the first bite. By eating more carefully, if we are happy, we can eat better, stabilize and stop eating. It also helps us to give up emotional or stressful food. The first step towards healthier choices to feed our food is to learn more about and understand the food we eat.

Conscious food has a positive effect on our health. Studies have shown that deliberately eating or slowing down eating can help in weight management, diabetes care and positive outcomes for men with prostate cancer that changes their diet. The more we become aware of what we eat, when what we eat, and how much we eat, we can identify unhealthy habits and behaviors that prevent us from making healthy decisions. With this awareness, we can begin to change our behavior and leave unhealthy patterns that no longer serve us.

Exercise of Mindful Eating: Taste the Mindfulness By Taking Just a Bite

I chose a refreshing fresh organic strawberry for this thought exercise. You can choose a comfortable meal to your liking.

Breathing:

Take a deep breath and share. Monitor all ideas and try to drop any comments you have in this exercise. Try to wake up innocent curiosity.

Search:

Place the strawberries in your hand and watch them before you eat them first. See the clear colors of strawberries. Note the small veins around the seeds around the circular and soft curves, and you can feel the green leaves around the stems. Enjoy how the sun and rain nourish the plants of this small berry and how it provides nutrients.

Taste:

Place the strawberries on your lips and you will find that you are waiting for the first bite. Note that you feel good before taking the first bite. Has your mouth started to flow? If so, please note that this is the beginning of the digestion process. Our body prepares food for the first bite. Ask yourself, "Am I hungry?"

First Bite:

Take a piece of strawberries carefully. Check the consistency of mouth and mouth before chewing. Is it sweet, juicy, sour?

Slowly Eat the Food:

Start slowly chewing the strawberries. How does the bait change? Is it more intense? What type of thoughts, emotions and physical feelings that appear when chewing your first mouth slowly. Pay attention to their comfort. Try the taste. Attention to the next bite may be interested in the desire to swallow.

Swallow:

When finished, swallow this first mouth. Can you understand the idea of swallowing how to create it? Swallowing is usually unconscious and spontaneous. Focus on your thoughts, feelings and feelings. Enjoy how these berries provide all the important nutrients to your body

Focus on Eating:

Be careful to eat strawberries. Note the difference between the second, third, and fourth ports. When did you start to feel happy, satisfied and satisfied? While eating this week, continue to take up these wonderful principles. Even a good meal is a good start. You do not have to spend too much time on each bite, but trying to pay attention to each meal is a great experience. This exercise should be cultivated for a long time. Each conscious experience enhances your skills. Over time, a conscious diet is natural and promotes a healthy body and mind choices.

Nourish Happiness with Mindful Eating:

Cultivating happiness and well-being in good times - for example, enjoying tasty food - helps us build resilience and emotional strength during these difficult times.

Want to be happy? I know I'll be very happy, and I'm sure people next to me will be very happy. Everyone will be very happy. Desire is part of our biology and it is deeply rooted in our brains. But the causes of happiness are varied and complex. Many people think you are very lucky. But luck is not something, so it will never be lost. Happiness is an experience, in which case you can experience happiness. There are four ways to do this, and a conscious diet can improve the happiness that surrounded it.

Four types of happiness that can be used through diet

1) Sensory Communication Good Luck (Shape, Taste, Sensation, Sensation, Touch and Ring)

The easiest and most obvious way to take care of your happiness is to allow you to accept rich sensory enjoyment by giving up food. When you notice the beauty of food, take a deep breath and taste your food. Pay attention to the food in the mouth or to the touch of the fork in the mouth or voice in the mouth when chewing. We were given the opportunity! Come on, jump to the sensory enjoyment to eat!

2) **Happiness in a Positive State of Mind (Happiness, Compassion, Compassion and Balance)**

Life is full of stress and challenges, the ability to empathize and the patient during these difficult periods is a special gift. You can begin to practice seeing happiness because when you stop

living and look for "good" attitudes, you will find that these emotional fixations are easier to deal with difficult situations. Be happy when you have useful ideas!

You can begin to practice seeing happiness because when you stop living and look for "good" attitudes, you will find that these emotional fixations are easier to deal with difficult situations.

3) **Focus on Happiness (Focus on Ideas and Ideas for One Project)**

Method 3 is the focus rather than sharing. If you allow yourself to focus on one thing, one project, one experience, typical chat and distraction around you, you will begin to calm down and be free to focus on future tasks. Creating a way to focus and attract attention is a valuable gift for planning your life. Focus your thoughts and thoughts on the tasks ahead.

4) Good Luck (Shared Experience and Humanity as Part of Human Experience)

The fourth way to estimate happiness is to lose any expectations. For example, the idea of eating consciously can help you do "X" or "Y". Do not be fooled tomorrow. Maintain the status quo; enjoy the miracle of consciousness, the rise of wisdom, and the excitement that arises when consciously eating. Hello, people of insight.

If you think about it, the best way to eat is to exercise the ability to see happiness and pleasure every day! If you constantly feed these four types of happiness in a comfortable life, every moment will be more interesting. At the same time, it enhances emotional strength and adaptability when life is difficult.

Mindful Eating Makes the Heart Happy:

The human heart is a wonderful muscle that can pull about 5 liters of blood a day. Minutes in your body, about 2000 liters of blood a day! The average heart even exceeds 100,000 times a day. Therefore, it makes sense to do everything possible to grow and maintain a strong and healthy heart.

Did you know that the food you eat will directly affect your heart health? Doctors agree that improving diet can improve overall health and help you overcome current health problems such as high cholesterol, high blood pressure and high blood sugar. And prevent future health problems. Foods in your heart include four foods: fat, sodium, sugar and fiber.

It is important to know that there are healthy and unhealthy fats. A healthy heart diet contains moderate amounts of unsaturated and multiple unsaturated fatty acids, especially those containing omega-3 fatty acids such as fish, shellfish, flaxseeds and some dairy products. Unhealthy fats, called saturated and unsaturated fatty acids, can be found in fried foods, packaged baked goods (especially glass) and snacks, as well as shellfish and pies.

Reduce meat, cheese, butter and cream. Go find more vegetable fat. For example, add guacamole instead of cheese to tacos. Sprinkle peanut butter instead of butter in the morning ceremony. Use a teaspoon of olive oil instead of a piece of butter to fry the vegetables.

Reducing sodium intake daily is also critical to heart health. Americans use about 4,000 mg of sodium per day. One day, twice the recommended number.

Follow these simple steps to reduce sodium intake: 1) Avoid salts and salts. 2) Avoid processed foods such as canned foods, meat, biscuits, fried potatoes and even frozen foods. 3) Choose to eat more at home to avoid foods that usually contain too much sodium to increase the flavor.

Let's talk now about sweet things. Sugar is a threat to heart health because it increases blood sugar levels and stimulates insulin production. This leads to many problems in patients with diabetes, diabetes and metabolic syndrome. Foods with high sugar content usually contain a lot of calories, which can lead to excessive consumption and a significant increase in weight, which eventually leads to obesity.

A healthy diet of the heart contains carbohydrates, even a small amount of sugar - in the form and quantity is limited. Sticking to fruits, vegetables, whole grains, milk and milk because these foods contain sugars, natural vitamins, minerals and essential carbohydrates - the main source of energy for the body.

Finally, try to keep your heart healthy by including fruits and vegetables - at least five servings a day - and whole grains in your diet. Some tips to remember: 1) Fresh fruit contains more fiber than canned food. 2) eat as much peel as possible. 3) Eat whole fruit instead of juice. 4) Use vegetable slices as afternoon food 4) choose a salad instead of French fries at lunch. 5) Cook with whole wheat flour. 6) Prepare brown rice instead of white rice for family meals.

A combination of thoughtful food and moderate intensity exercise is the best formula for gentle heart health. What are you waiting for? Start a health trip today.

Chapter 3

Best Ways to Practice Mindful Eating

Some Ways to Eat Mindfully:

For many of us, it is unrealistic to exercise extreme caution or educate awareness, especially for family, work, and many distractions around us. Except for our friends, our family and colleagues have no patience to eat with us because we eat five minutes at a time. So be sympathetic and ask yourself if you are officially aware of going out and special occasions, and whether you are eating informal food in your daily life.

Diet is an important part of everyday life. However, you rarely spend time enjoying the food. For many of us, busy life means that we can eat as much as possible: in front of the computer around the conference table - almost everywhere, except on the table. Eating in our community is often a useless task, not an enjoyable and nutritious experience. Unhealthy foods and excessive care can have negative health effects on indigestion and obesity. On the other hand, a mindful diet promotes digestion, supports nutrient uptake, increases the ideal body weight, and helps you build healthy relationships with your diet.

Mindful eating is not a diet. This is a mindful way to eat and enjoy health and happiness. A mindful diet is to make the eating experience cautious and grateful. By slowing down and monitoring the way you eat in food and food, you are more likely to make better choices to feed your body. Here are some guidelines for exercising mindful eating.

What I want to present in this hall is what I call food awareness, perhaps a deliberate "informal" food option, not a formal mindful eating option. During the period of madness, tension, and extra food on holidays, this year spanned the new Halloween, where we ate more recklessly than thought-provoking. Here are some simple guidelines to remember to distinguish between food and due diligence (more), which makes our body and mind.

Here are some ways to eat mindfully:

1) Let Your Body Hold Your Mind:

Eat quickly, ignore the body signal. When your body tells you it's full, you eat and stop.

Minimizing the best ways to get the body and mind to deliver the food we really need. The body actually sends a saturated signal to the brain about it. 20 minutes, why often eat unconsciously. But as we slow down, you can give your body a chance to grab your mind and hear the right amount of signals. The easiest way to slow down is to sit and eat, 25 times time (or more often), put a fork between the bites and all the old ways that look less useful. How can you delay your meal and monitor your body signals better?

2) Know the Signal Of Personal Hunger in the Body:

Do you respond to emotional or physical needs?

Often we listen to our initial thoughts, but as with many mind exercises, we can find more wisdom by first focusing on our bodies. Is your stomach low, is your energy low or a bit dizzy? Often, when you decide our minds, we prefer to eat from our bodies. Careful nutrition means listening deeply to the cult signals of our bodies. Ask yourself: What kind of signals your body sends, and what causes your mood for hunger?

3) Create a Healthy Eating Environment:

Eat alone and eat randomly, eat with others at certain times and places.

Another way to think without thinking is to go to the buffet and eat at times instead of actively thinking about our meals and snacks. On the one hand, it slows down, but it prevents us from developing healthy environmental indicators, what we eat and what we eat, and directing the brain to get new food signals that are not always perfect. (Do you really want to eat your habits every time you take the bus or in other situations?) Of course, we will eat something from time to time, but it can be your mind and your own health. Improve your body, do not forget your mood and help plan your sleep, eat in times and places constantly changing. Yes, that means you sit at a table and eat on a plate or a bowl, do not take food out of the container and use tools that are not in our hands. It also helps to eat with others. Not only want to share and maintain a healthy relationship, but you also want to slow down and enjoy more food and entertainment; we can advise our partners without eating too much or too little food.

If we store food in cabinets and refrigerators, we may eat more healthy and healthy foods. So think about what is nearby, where it is and whether it is in front of you. If we limit our food to kitchens and restaurants, we are also less likely to eat without thinking or doing multiple tasks.

For several reasons, the grapes you eat are very strong. One reason is that when we reduce our activities and eat healthy foods like raisins, we often prefer them instead of our stories about healthy foods. Eat it.

You do not have to plan carefully to eat for each bite, so stay flexible, especially on special occasions. But remember that you can change your eating habits in different seasons or on different occasions. If you plan, it is more likely to eat the amount your body needs, instead of eating or eating too much after eating a bit, then regretting.

Even if you are hungry, the classic advice is not buying, but it is also in the middle. The psychological effect known as "moral license" suggests that buyers who buy bald heads tend to go to liquids or ice rooms instead of those who do not. We seem to believe that our karma is straight, and we can "use it" in fast food or other desired behaviors.

4) Understand Your Motivation:

Emotional calm food compared to nutritious food.

This is another difficult balance; ideally, we find that nourishing foods are satisfactory and soothing. But think again in this first mindful grape. Would you like to try it before? For several reasons, the grapes you eat are very strong. One reason is that when we reduce our activities and eat healthy foods like raisins, we often prefer them instead of our stories about healthy foods. Eat it. By eating a more varied healthy diet, we can enjoy more comfortable food faster, but more likely to enjoy healthy eating. Finally, we noticed that many foods are satisfying spiritually and physically and not just.

5) Connect Deeper With Food:

Consider the food source instead of the finished product. Unless you are a fisherman, a collector or a farmer, we will separate more and more from food. Many of us did not even think of a meal outside the supermarket packaging. This is a shame because food offers a wonderful opportunity to build deeper relationships with nature, elements and each other.

When we no longer see all the people who share your food, those dear ones (and those who are already ready) give the people who are already in the shelves, who planted and harvested them. It is difficult for people who support them to be both grateful and communicative. When you sit and eat what you eat, pay attention to water, land and other elements that help in training. You can think about the cultural traditions of the food you bring, the recipes that your friends have generously shared, or the recipes you bring from far away and distant times. Yeah.

Look at everything in the meal, it becomes an effort, all the people who give them time and energy, the cosmic elements that contribute, the friends or grandparents who share the recipes, even those who share their time and the efforts that transformed them and who transformed themselves into life is gratitude to the living beings of this meal. By being more vigilant, we can begin to make better choices about the sustainability and health of our food, not only for ourselves but for the whole planet.

6) Be Careful With Your Plate:

Multitasking and eating recipes do not provide insight into your physical needs and requirements. We all went through the experience of going to the cinema using a bag of popcorn, and before the end of the next attraction, we wanted to know who ate all the popcorn. When distracted, it becomes difficult to hear signals about our bodies and other needs of food. Try to do a job during the next meal, eat easily, not excrete or distract your attention, and not just enjoy the company you are talking to.

When we look at formal and mindful eating habits with the observation of our decline or decline, the reality is that we live and eat in the real world, a busy place. But we can take advantage of the knowledge we get from official practice: cut down, listen to our bodies, do one, do small- scale rituals, consider what we often eat and more informal attention.

7) Cut And Remove the Plug:

Food sometimes looks like something else in the to-do list. When you have a chance, do you drive to eat? Or take time to sit down and eat, but watch television blindly and ignore what you eat or eat. Have you ever eaten the aquarium and want to know how to complete the next task quickly? Guess what? Your body and mind need rest; they need food to feel the supplement.

Avoid watching TV and making phone calls or text messages while eating. Stop working and stay away from your computer. Take everything aside, take a break and enjoy your food. Focus on your meal

When you sit down to eat - without intervention - see your food and learn how to eat it. You can develop bad habits to eat very quickly, or you can eat them without tasting the food. Because during the real rest period, you will be stimulated with a precise diet, and you can feel comfortable and focused throughout the day.

8) Eat Slowly:

When you are full, your brain needs time to notice that you are eating and communicating with your body. It takes about 20 minutes for the brain to know that you have enough food. Rest between bites can promote a healthy and slow diet.

Put your fork between primitives. Stop eating in your mouth before proceeding to the next day. When you eat with friends or family, you will increase your conversions. Do not try to please yourself. To satisfy

In this way, eating slowly helps prevent over-eating, resulting in unnecessary weight gain and digestive pressure.

9) Chew Well:

Eating on the road can cause chewing and chewing undigested food particles through the colon. These particles can cause unpleasant symptoms such as flatulence, gas and indigestion.

Make food carefully until it becomes soft and fragile. Some experts recommend chewing 30 to 50 times at a time. Saliva is rich in active enzymes that help break food. The longer the food is salted for long (by chewing), the easier it is to move it in the intestines.

Good chewing stimulates the digestive process and improves the absorption of vitamins and nutrients. Good digestion is necessary for public health.

10) Sip, Do Not Swallow:

However, you can drink plenty of water while eating, soften stomach acid and digest slowly.

Reduce fluid consumption for 15 minutes before eating and after at least 15 to 30 minutes of eating. If you prefer to drink while eating, take a small tube. Peppermint and lemon juice are digested.

If your system is full of excess fluids, you can prevent or reduce gas and blowing. You may find it easier after eating.

11) Incubate Your Senses:

Mindful eating can be a magical and exciting experience. There are many things in the food that you can see and experience - color, texture, taste and sound. Food is more than just taste. If you want to talk to all the senses, this is a great way to fully appear in the meal.

Please note the color and shape of the food for the next meal. Then close your eyes and feel the taste of food. What kind of sound do you hear when you close your eyes? When chewing, pay attention to taste and texture.

If you take the time to get to know and enjoy the taste and color of the food, you are surprised by the outstanding performance of some sensory experiences. When you eat your senses while eating, you will also be encouraged to slow down and enjoy a full meal experience.

12) Eat Only When You Are Hungry:

Easy to sneak into a senseless or passionate snacks activity, or think you need a certain amount of food every day. But if you eat a lot of snacks between meals, you will feel very satisfied, or find that you are not hungry when you eat. If you are not hungry, eating may make you feel guilty later, if you eat too much. Of course, if you are hungry, the healthy snacks between meals can be enjoyable and nutritious.

Listen to your body. Is your stomach stiff? Do you feel empty or dizzy? Are you thirsty if you are already hungry, have snacks or eat them? Do not wait until you feel hungry and do not eat because you eat. When eating snacks, ask yourself why you should eat.

Eat only when you feel hungry and remind you that your body needs energy and needs to maintain your health. In order to avoid emotional diet and unnecessary snacks, these harmful feelings should be taken while eating. You can prevent excess weight when you hunger.

13) Express Grateful Attitude:

Check the time and work required to prepare meals. Take a moment to look at all ingredients, prepare your food and bring it to your dish. Spend some time enjoying the nutritious and enjoyable food you'll enjoy right away. Give the blessing or rest before eating to achieve your happiness. Thank you very much for preparing this meal.

Everyone appreciates their work and commitment; we appreciate food and remember how people and others communicate to support nutritious food. This simple assertion can help you enjoy your clothes and satisfaction.

Attention to diet is a natural and enjoyable experience that promotes good health. Your body will fully benefit from the slowdown and appearance with the meal. Not only is it important for you to eat, but also how to eat.

14) Start Eating:

It takes time to develop new habits. It may be always difficult to develop a mindful habit of eating, but you can only eat one meal or even one meal. Be aware of hunger and eating habits before eating, or adjust to satiety at the end of the meal - these are good ways to attract attention

15) Remove Interference from View:

Place the phone in another room or turn it off completely. Turn off your TV and computer and save everything that makes you away from the dining experience - books, magazines, and newspapers.

Focus on food in front of you.

16) Adjust Your View

Pay attention to your mind when you start this exercise. Explain that there is no right or wrong way to eat, but there is another level of awareness of the eating experience. Focus on eating feeling. When you notice that your thoughts have been lost, you must carefully bring them back to the dining experience.

17) Take Your Time:

You should delay a mindful diet, so digestive hormones can tell your mind that you are full before eating too much. Closing the fork between bites is a good way to start. In addition, you can enjoy a better dining experience, especially if you are with your loved ones.

18) Chew 25 Times:

Chewing may be the easiest and most effective way to develop healthy eating habits. The whole diet movement, led by the late Horace Fletcher, is based on more chewing to help reduce the idea. Although Fletcher has taken this idea a step forward (and perhaps insane), reliable scientific data suggest that additional chewing can reduce total food consumption.

I recommend 25 here, but chewing another feature. The most important thing is to choose a number and count your croquet until you reach them. The figures themselves are not very consistent.

Remind you to chew my iPhone application as "Memories". Spray a few minutes before the usual meal, simply remind you to chew it 25 times

19) Feed Yourself with Non-Dominant Hands:

This is a good way to force you to pay attention to what you are doing. An easy way is to force you to eat with a non-dominant hand, which represents 90% of the left hand. There may be a lot of things to do for each meal, but the experience of breakfast and snacks is a good start.

But be aware that if you become very good, you can return to your arrogant habits.

20) Eat With Chopsticks for a Whole Week:

Even if you are growing chopsticks as the main tool, you may not use them on sandwiches or a bag of chips.

One day, I learned from a local technology company that a group of employees asked for a stick for a week of mindful exercise. Despite their failure, however, the goal was not everything, they were all moved in the office away, and many results changed their life reports.

When someone discovers that chopsticks prevent him from experiencing his favorite ritual, it usually develops in the morning. It is clear that the taste of bread is not as attractive as bread objects.

When he realized that he did not want to eat bread, he did not decide.

21) Place the Fork Between the Bites:

Putting a fork between bites is an excellent complement to chew. When you close the fork, focus on chewing the food instead of taking it off the dish and eating. It also encourages you to slow down and pay more attention to the taste of food instead of creating it as soon as possible.

22) Close Your Eyes and Eat the First Bite:

When I went to a restaurant, the whole cooking experience, including the culinary experience on our table, continued in the dark. Our idea is to focus on the dining experience without disturbing the point of view. Unfortunately, the food in this restaurant is terrible, and its emphasis makes it more obvious. But this is a good lesson; I did not try to eat too much food.

It is impractical to eat all meals in the dark even with your eyes closed. If you take the time to experience all of your attention, you can eat the rest of the meal more consciously. Focus on all odors and their interactions in the mouth, as well as the smell and texture. This will help you enjoy food and eat more slowly.

23) Try to Identify Each Ingredient in Your Food:

Trying to taste and identify different ingredients in your meal is another great way to focus on your moments and eat more carefully. This is especially useful for restaurants that you have not prepared for yourself. Another advantage of this technique is that they make you more creative in the kitchen.

24) Place the Food on the Dish:

This seems obvious, but eating in a bag is not a very delicate exercise. Usually, develop snacks and small desserts on a plate before eating. You need to clarify what to eat and how much you eat.

General Principles of Mindful Eating:

"General principles of mindful diet, awareness of nutrients that prepare and consume food, to choose healthy and nutritious foods, to define food preferences with integrity and appreciation, to show signs of physical hunger and hunger to prevent wisdom and cooking from losing wisdom." - Cheryl Harris, MPH, RD

If you have a busy modern lifestyle, please allow time to adapt to your needs. It moves constantly from one to the other, ignoring what your body or mind really wants. Attention can help you understand this.

By applying to mindful eating, you can help identify patterns and behaviors, as well as physical evidence of hunger and bloating.

Attention when eating can help you focus on the present, rather than maintaining normal and unsatisfactory behavior. Food awareness is a way to look inside, to learn more about your relationship with food and you can use it to eat happily.

The body contains a lot of knowledge and information. If you're thinking about dining, you can make informed decisions, not automatic behavior, and often stop feeling. Once you understand these habits, you can change your behavior better.

Encourage people who deliberately choose food and nutrition:

- Explore their inner wisdom about food preferences and hate
- Choose the food that attracts and nourishes the body
- Accept some food preferences without judgment or self-criticism
- Realize that the exercise signal from your body begins to eat and stop eating
- It must be clear that eating habits and eating experience are unique.

Here are general principles of mindful eating:

The correct way of thinking about eating is based on the principles of Rebecca G. Frei and Laura Jean Cataldo, RN:

- Listen to hunger and satiety inside the body
- Select a personal stimulus to eat without thinking about it. For example, social pressure, strong emotions and certain foods

- Quality is higher than the amount of food
- Estimate emotional value or fun and food

Exercising mindfulness in a busy world can sometimes be a challenge, but you can find ways to adjust your body more easily by understanding and implementing these basic principles and practices. You will be pleasantly surprised to see how your relationship with food can change better and that this can have a significant impact on your overall health and well-being.

Chapter # 4

Benefits of Mindful Eating

Remember that food is no longer a secret! If you've read the New York Times article, "Thinking about food," "Thinking about food," you might be "hungry" about how to eat this healthy and healing way. The system uses mindfulness or current art to treat modern eating disorders. This is not a diet; there are no menu or dietary restrictions. Develop a new way of thinking about food.

The good news is that a healthy diet can help to consume a lot of food and other nutritional problems. In the past 20 years, studies have shown that deliberate eating can help you (1) reduce over-eating; 2) lose weight and reduce body mass index (BMI) 3) treat chronic eating disorders such as anorexia and bulimia Sickness and reduce anxiety about food and body, 4) Improved symptoms of type 2 diabetes. Advantage!

Intuitively, mindful food is useful for overeating. It slows down your speed, informs you of size, and helps you overcome negative and automatic eating habits such as over-eating while watching your favorite programs. How can this help other people solve other problematic eating habits?

In short, if you eat too much or your diet is strict, you probably forgot your hunger and your money. This separation must be cured between body and mind. Mindful food usually contains three types of help:

1) A careful diet brings you back to your body and allows you to know when to stop and eat. If your hunger and wealth are distorted or distorted by too much food, diet or comfort, this may be a daunting task.

2) Alertness can control your emotions Sometimes people limit or eat too much to deal with negative emotions. Eating and not eating can distract your attention. For example, if you are healthier about this issue. For example, through breathing and anxiety gently, you may not be able to control your feelings through eating habits. They can bear their feelings, no matter how satisfied they are; they will not push back or fill the food.

3) Mindful eating will change the way you believe. Rather than responding to food ideas that make you eat too much, your diet or your emotional system. I have interacted so much with these ideas. You can hear these ideas without having to follow them.

Benefits of Mindful Eating:

In today's fast-paced and technology-based society, we face a busy schedule and long hours of work or study. You can do a lot of things, and your planners can list grocery stores and tasks that you need to do all day to help you forget or have lunch. Sometimes when we are too busy, forget to eat, or when we have the opportunity, we do not have time to enjoy our food. Do we get enough nutrients, vitamins, carbohydrates, fats and other essentials; do our bodies need to be happy and healthy? Some of us cast food very quickly, so we still feel hungry after eating. In fact, we do not have enough time to absorb the facts we have dealt with, and we have a sense of hunger constantly because our brains always think we are hungry. Conscience is a practice of meditation and awareness. This is a Buddhist concept that helps us knows what to eat when we eat, why we eat and enjoy the food we eat. By eating consciously, we can change our eating habits and understand what we eat and absorb in our bodies, and how we get the right nutrients from our diet.

Reduce Stress and Anxiety:

If you eat wisely, you will be more aware of what you feel about food. Do you eat because you have stress at work or are you afraid of future exams? By spending time eating and focusing on your feelings, you can direct your emotional roots and learn to control your emotions. The cognitive therapy program developed by John Kabat Zein and his colleagues showed that anxiety and symptoms of depression decreased significantly in patients with a generalized anxiety disorder (GAD).

Many studies have shown that mindful can not only help an individual overcome stress but also reduces overall stress. Mindfulness can help to improve mood regulation and mental state, to help us manage stress (REMMERS, Topolinksi and Koole, 2016).

Mindfulness also develops more active coping strategies in stressful situations, including management mode and risk reduction to avoid (Donald Watkins, 2016).

It Can Help You Manage Your Emotions:

Do you find that you eat too much or do not eat at all because of overwhelming emotions? Maybe something happened, you are angry or sad, so I decided to go to the store to drink some fast food. Mindful eating can help you control your feelings and spend time chewing food and looking for smell, taste and consistency. If you know more about your food intake, it will be more adaptable to your health. Are you unhappy, happy or angry? Remember when you eat next.

Reduce Excess Food and Diet Attacks:

There are many people who eat or eat too much, be it stress or laziness. Obesity A pandemic is very important in today's society. Food awareness and meditation can reduce bad habits associated with over-chewing food slowly and eat for at least 20 minutes. In this way, you can give your brain enough time to process the substance you have taken, and you have enough time to properly absorb the body. Mental meditation studies have been evaluated as possible evidence of treatment for weight loss, stress and behaviors associated with food attacks.

Treatment of Chronic Eating Disorders:

Some people suffer from chronic eating disorders such as anorexia and bulimia. It is known that people with bulimia eat too much, so waste their food, and patients with anorexia tend to reduce their consumption. By knowing how to eat and you can help people with chronic eating disorders to focus on foods you eat, such as carbohydrates, protein, vitamins, etc., by following these steps, the nutrients that your body needs. This way, you get used to relaxing, so you do not have to suffer from eating disorders like anorexia and bulimia. A case study was conducted in which a 19-year-old girl was helped and showed a decrease in overall dietary restriction.

Help Find Your Body:

If you are aware, you will also send a signal to your body that you should tell you when to start eating and when to stop eating. Once your body knows the direction, it tells you when to start eating or stopping. This can help you by wasting your food or forgetting what you should.

Helps With Food Portion:

Mindful eating can help you understand how much food you put in your body and learn more about how much food you eat. This helps to reduce excess food. By knowing your food, be sure to eat all the protein, carbohydrates and other substances your body needs to maintain good health. You can also read HFR articles in the top 10 tips to manage your share!

Enhanced Focus:

If you take the time to eat well and eat well, you should also pay attention. This can help you avoid outside interference in your daily life and increase your concentration and focus on other things.

Mental Health and Other Benefits

Mindful eating can also promote mental health. Different foods can directly affect our emotional state (Kidwell & Hasford, 2014). So, when you are close to food, you can better control your emotional health.

Other benefits of mindful eating can be:

- Identify emotional and interactive eating habits that lead to poor emotional health.
- Feed the body, heart, mind and soul.
- Understand your relationship with food and the wider environment.
- Better control and responsibility for making informed and positive decisions.

Ability to Deal Better with Disease:

Many studies have focused on the use of mindful eating in cancer patients and patients with chronic or incurable diseases. Similarly, some studies on stress and anxiety reduction awareness (Zernicke et al., 2016), and other studies link awareness and reduce the number of cancer patients and caregivers together with ruminants (Labelle et al., 2015). In general, it has been shown that mindful eating helps patients focus more on improving their quality of life and beyond physical pain (Garland and Howard, 2013).

Support Recovery:

Mindfulness not only helps patients control the disease but also recovers. Studies have shown that breast cancer survivors who exercise mindfulness have more empathy and less stress (Boyle et al., 2017). After binding the mind, meditation and yoga promote the growth of invasive breast cancer survivors, while reducing anxiety during rehabilitation (Tamagawa et al., 2015)

Symptoms Associated with Depression and Anxiety:

Exercise of self-control helps to control emotional responses better (Brown et al., 2007). When depression and anxiety identify and identify a powerful emotional tool without accepting it as the only truth or deviate from experience, which may be useful (Costa and Barnhofer, 2016).

Prevent In Binge Eating:

If you have problems with bulimia, you will feel helpless. Fortunately, mindful eating exercises can help. Some studies have shown that mindfulness helps to reduce the onset of eating attacks and emotional diets.

The next time you want to eat or eat, sit on the table. Try to eat slowly and carefully. You may not eat too much or do not feel guilty in the future. Avoid eating on the couch!

Teach You To Live As a Gift:

Living now is very important, especially if you want to be happier. Studies have shown that people are happier now, rather than leaving their thoughts behind. Mindful food can help you pay more attention during the day.

Mindful Eating Can Help Clean Things Up:

Although factors such as hormones and inflammation affect weight loss, over-eating is still the main reason people reach. By avoiding over-eating, you can easily reach your weight goals.

Can Prevent Stomach Bloating:

Did you know that fast food can cause soft feelings and indigestion? If you eat quickly, you will breathe a lot of air, making you feel bloated and uncomfortable.

The more you eat the less air you swallow. By chewing, the food is cut into small pieces, making it easier to digest and absorb nutrients.

You Can Learn To Enjoy Healthy Food:

We are ready to believe that fast food is delicious and tasteless. After a slowdown, you'll find that junk food is not as tasty as you think, healthy food tastes good.

You Can Start To Believe More And Eat:

If they do not control their passion, I usually advise people to take out all the junk food from home. You may not have to do this when you start eating healthy. No matter how many options you have, you can count on healthy options.

More Fun in Social Activities:

If you have good food, social activities will become more interesting than ever. You do not have to worry about enjoying a lot of fun because you decide what to eat and how much you eat. Use these tips to eat well in social activities.

Control Your Weight:

One of the most prominent benefits is weight loss. Sensitive dietary choices are related to weight management and weight loss for overweight men (Dalen et al., 2010). Even trying to report that women often eat at restaurants may be more difficult (Timmerman and Brown, 2012).

If you improve your old eating habits by eating slowly, chewing 20 to 40 times and maintaining your taste and persistence, you can also exercise controls in yourself. This control helps reduce fat and thus lose weight.

Another study found that people who ate more precise food said they ate fewer calories to beat weight better (Bishara, Hutchinson and Wilson, 2013).

Unlike natural diets that can cause difficulties, diets encourage you to consciously focus on the physical needs of your diet and the negative effects on your body and your mind if you eat too much.

As I said before, mindful eating is more than just losing weight. Of course, in the end, you begin to improve your eating habits, and overall may take care of your weight. As you prepare for your body's needs and stop the stress or emotional diet, you will naturally begin to improve your eating habits. This may be the best side effect of the mind when we eat!

Whether you want to lose weight quickly, eat too much or do not eat unhealthily, you will lose the signs of real hunger and satiety. If you eat without thinking, you will not be able to meet your physical needs or ignore a range of healthy foods that focus on your actual calorie needs or stress. This may mean that a lot of manufactured parts or "comfortable foods" tend to be too heavy and increase your weight. But for some people, if they do not care about food, they will eat very little or too little food.

No matter how you ignore your body's signs and the need for healthy food, it can cause weight fluctuations and health problems. Unhealthy weight gain due to an inability to recognize or respond to processed foods can increase the risk of diabetes, obesity and various diseases. Eating, not eating breakfast, or limiting some foods other than healthy foods will not give you enough calories or nutrition, which is also harmful.

The good news is that if you are a person who needs to lose weight, it is likely to help you wake up. Awareness training is increasingly integrated into weight loss programs to promote changes in eating habits and exercise. Studies have shown that the higher the degree of awareness testing, the higher the weight and unhealthy obesity.

As part of the NutriNet-Santé study of 2015, researchers at the Center for Nutrition Research at the University of Paris monitored and supervised and monitored 14,400 men and 49,228 women under the age of 18. Use a five-part questionnaire to collect self-reported, self-reported, and self- reported data. The results showed that the most sensitive women were less likely to gain weight and excess weight. The older the lighter, although this bond is too heavy and not focused enough to be important.

As I read, psychological and cognitive processes have a significant impact on food consumption. A further systematic review of 19 clinical studies on weight loss exercise in 2015 showed that most of them contributed to weight loss. Eight randomized controlled trials were assessed to determine the impact of awareness-based interventions on the weight of people trying to lose weight. In eight studies published in peer-reviewed journals, there is six reported significant weight loss in weight to change the way of thinking of the disease (report no significant change, another report no weight, which means that the results may be more powerful.

Reduce Stress When Eating:

Stress can spoil your diet and fitness goals. Everyone is linked to an emotional diet. This is part of the people! We all love food, enjoy different types of food, and find comfort in our favorite dishes. But some people can control the natural desire to eat better food than others by discovering that they sometimes combine comfortable diets into other healthy meals.

Turning off a passionate diet can seriously affect your weight and health because it ends the vicious circle. Awareness can help you avoid a stressful diet because it teaches you to respond to situations rather than simply respond to them. They recognize your wishes but do not have to control them automatically or through them.

If you are more in tune with your feelings and know how your choices work, stop eating and eat more realistic portions when you are full. If you are aware of the effects of stress, you can end the spontaneous behavior that leads to agility - making many people feel embarrassed and even nervous!

You may have seen that chronic stress can affect the quality of your life. Include eating habits associated with grazing stress, persistent snacks, or the desire to eat chocolate and other carbohydrates or the desire to eat sugar. Stop the bike by thinking about the food needs before satisfying them, leading to guilt and over-eating.

More Satisfied with Food:

Mindful eating will remind you of your body's signs and senses. With a careful diet, you can focus on your diet again without losing control. Although finding satisfaction with food seems to reverse results. But the more we realized we needed less to eat!

Think about it: If you eat something savory every second, like a hot chocolate cake, you usually eat a few bites. You realize that everything is fine, you realize how much you eat, and you always have a chance to eat something new. But you cannot finish the painting because it is in front of you, even if you feel full or guilty or say, "This is my only chance to eat."

No Need to Eat Anymore:

If you take the right amount, please follow the diet. Standard plans and plans do not usually work long term because they do not teach you how to control your feelings and preferences because food groups are not excluded or starved. In the long term, this is what you do, not what you enter and get out of, which allows you to listen to your body, not just external advice.

Mindful eating can significantly reduce over-eating habits directly associated with obesity. Excessive obesity is a common symptom in people with obsessive-compulsive disorder. Scientists report that mind has an inhibitory effect on auto responder and can also improve cognitive, behavioral and emotional resilience, especially for individuals with obsessive- compulsive disorder. A study report suggests that it is better to control diets by learning new habits rather than learning punishment-based reflection in patients with obsessive-compulsive disorder. In addition, the exercise of the mindful eating is also expected to improve behavioral flexibility, increase self-esteem and reduce stress levels.

Best Prevent and Manage Health Problems:

Some studies have shown that deliberate food training can improve self-management of diseases such as diabetes, gastrointestinal problems and eating disorders. A special nutrition plan is needed. Published in the Danish Journal of Veterinary Medicine and Food Administration in 2013.

You can better control the behavioral care of the most vulnerable people and decide to meet your particular needs. In other words, mindful eating is a free natural cure for diabetes because diabetics become what they eat, why they eat and what they can do to change it. When they pay more attention to their habits, they can better control eating and blood sugar levels.

Awareness-based methods have become more common, such as eating disorders such as eating, anorexia, or food addiction. A study conducted by the Department of Behavioral Sciences at Rush University Medical Center in 2014 showed that 14 mindfulness exercises were conducted and that eating disorders training had positive results. Mindfulness helps to reduce the bulimia, emotional feelings and/or unhealthy weight changes of people who participate in these harmful behaviors.

Mindful Eating Improving Eating Habits:

Through fine eating habits, the taste is extended and the taste experience is improved. This is particularly useful for tired consumers who can add more nutrients and foods to their diet. Mindful eating is also linked to the destruction of eating habits. A study by Canadian teenagers found that conservative eating habits significantly reduced the use of automatic snacks and reduced the chances of students choosing healthy snacks rather than unhealthy snacks. Reducing unhealthy eating habits and increasing the consumption of healthy foods such as fresh fruits can help improve physical and mental health and overcome cognitive stress.

To promote awareness, a group of overweight people were provided with training programs. One of the results of training is that mindful drinking can significantly reduce stress, which can lead to neurasthenia. It was also determined that mindful eating can increase self-esteem, increase concentration, and prevent participation in behaviors that lead to anxiety. It also helps to improve self-control to reduce unwanted food.

Chapter # 5

Get Rid Of Emotional Eating

What is Emotional Eating?

Emotional diets (or diet focus) are the cause of many food failure situations. We do not eat always just to satisfy physical hunger. Many of us use food to feel better - food to meet their emotional needs, stress or deal with unpleasant feelings such as grief, loneliness or boredom. You can take a pint of ice in a bad mood, ask for a pizza when you're bored, go home alone or after a hard day's work.

Using food or celebrating as a reward at times is not necessarily bad. But if food is your main emotional management mechanism - if the first impulse is to open the refrigerator, if you are stressed, angry, angry, lonely, tired or bored - you fall into an unhealthy cycle, the real feeling is or never treated with Problems. Emotional hunger cannot be filled with food. The food seems delicious right now, but the feeling of food still exists. You often feel worse than before because you've just consumed unnecessary calories.

No matter how well you feel about eating and feeling, you can make positive changes. You can find healthier ways to control your feelings, so be careful instead of eating without giving reasons to regain weight and stop emotional eating.

The Difference between Emotional and Physical Hunger:

Emotional hunger can be very intense, so it is easy to put into physical hunger. But you can look for paths that help to distinguish between physical hunger and emotional hunger.

Emotional hunger suddenly happens. I hit you right away and it seems you can not stop it. However, physical hunger is gradually increasing. The desire to eat is not too bad or immediately satisfied (unless you have eaten for a long time).

Emotional hunger requires some comfortable meals. When you are hungry, everything looks almost good, including healthy foods like vegetables. But hunger and thirst require fast food or sweets that cause immediate attacks. You think you need cheese or pizza, there's nothing else you can do.

Emotional hunger often leads to meaningless food. Before you know it, you've already eaten a whole bag of chips or a pint of ice without really caring out. If you eat because of physical hunger, you usually have a better understanding of what you do.

When you are full, emotional hunger is not satisfactory. They always eat more and eat so much that they have to feed them. But physical hunger should not be great. You will be satisfied when your stomach is full.

Emotional hunger is not in the stomach. Instead of the growing stomach or abdominal pain, you feel hungry is a need you cannot get rid of. They focus on some textures, tastes and smells.

Emotional hunger often leads to regret, guilt, or shame. If you eat to please your hunger, you will not feel guilty or ashamed, because you will give your body what you need. If you feel guilty after eating, it may be because you know you did not eat for nutritional reasons.

Counter Emotional Eating With Mindfulness:

Emotional food is incredibly common but often misunderstood. Have you ever eaten sweets or big fries after a hard day's work, often without taking a conscious decision? Do your diet plans fail immediately if you have relationship problems, financial worries or self-confidence?

If you think this picture sounds very familiar to you, you are not alone. Eating emotions can be a source of shame and frustration, but there are ways to overcome it. The trick is to learn more about your triggers and develop a deliberate diet model that replaces the old and destructive model of emotional eating. This guide can help you improve and learn how to put food in a more positive light.

Check Out and Take a Moment:

You can take certain steps to maximize your chances of reducing your emotional eating. The main goal is to develop a model to deliberately eat instead. We will guide you through the steps needed to become an attentive eatery. They are lighter than you think!

First, note that when we are hungry, the automatic reaction to food. So if you have abdominal pain, you will probably go straight to tea without thinking about it. When you learn to slow down by taking a step between feeling and action, you often stop eating emotionally.

Next time you're hungry, deliberately take a moment to ask yourself, "Am I physically or emotionally hungry?" If you are not sure, ask yourself if you have a condition of urge (a sign of emotional hunger). If you walk around a banana to get to a chocolate bar, you'll probably encounter an emotional and not a physical need. Also, ask yourself if hunger suddenly appeared. This immediacy is also common in emotional eating.

If, based on the above information, you find that you are hungry emotionally (and not physically), ask yourself, "What do I feel?"

This will help you understand why you are hungry emotionally and will allow you to think of other ways to meet your needs.

All these issues create a greater gap between the feeling of thirst for food and the right food. And over time, a deliberate choice of food should become the norm and not the exception

Write it down and identify Your Emotional Triggers:

Emotional food always has some triggers and it's hard to find them. Phase two of your stimulating diet plan is to identify triggers and make them tangible. You can use a laptop to create a "diary" or just take notes on your phone or computer. Regardless of the format, note the time, add a description of your feelings and understand why you feel it. If you fancy a particular type of food, note that too.

For example, you may find yourself feeling hungry at 3 pm and that you especially wanted fries. Then you can add that you are sad because you miss your old partner. Over time, templates will appear in your cookbook.

By using these templates you can create links between specific desires and specific emotional needs. The process can also help you discover the excellent tasks that you can actively work on. In the example above you can try to get back into the dating world why you are destroying your desire to talk or you are talking about the relationship in therapy.

Make a More Appropriate Decision For You:

The next part of a conscious food trip is to make a better decision. You are now suitable for what you have learned through self-reflection. If you follow the steps above to notice that you are hungry, you may want to breastfeed during breastfeeding, which reduces total calories and keeps you healthy. If not, you'll notice that you are not full today, you really have to cook. Based on your physical needs, this is a great way to deal with real physical hunger.

If you are hungry, you cannot always avoid eating alone. In these cases, your strategy is not to eat away from food, but to eat better.

Find an Alternative Dish:

Alternative foods can be found as a savior to combat emotional feelings.

A good way is to look at the dominant scent and continue from there. So, if you crave chocolate, what sweet and healthy things can you eat? The fruit is a clear choice. At the same time, replace the potato flavored chips with spice-free cornflowers.

In some cases, the food you eat is very close to the food you want and feels better. Then you can eat less and experience.

There is no automatic desire at all. In fact, you have "trained" your body and your mind and relied on food this way.

Look for Positive Activity to Drain Your Emotional Diet:

Although an alternative diet strategy may work, the best you can do is replace your emotional diet with healthy behavior. Going back to the nutrition diary, it's time to give your feedback a new dimension. When you write, try to find another way to make you feel better. Make sure they are positive, not just an unhealthy strategy.

For some people, personal relationships are different. Can you call a friend; make an appointment with your family, or even hug? For other people, it may be helpful to have another type of physical comfort. For example, try a luxury hot tub or candlelight or hug a blanket to watch a movie. Inspiration can also distract your emotional diet. In short, personal care plans or any kind of positive activity can help you, such as reading a success story, watching a TED conversation, or listening to motivational music.

Finally, even if it is not obvious, you can try training instead of eating. Feel good, reward your activities and increase your energy. There are many types of sports, so you will not have to keep up with the treadmill. Dancing, aquatic aerobics, riding and cycling are fun ways to experience emotions without losing calories.

Conscious Eating:

Most of us eat only in our mouths, but (as mentioned above), this is an important reason for over- eating. A way to develop positive habits of conscious and healthy eating in your daily life:

- Take a deep breath while you sit down to eat.
- Thank you for eating before you eat anything. This is not

necessarily a religious activity, though possible. Take some time to enjoy your happiness.

• Make sure you feel comfortable and have a good attitude.

• Chew food slowly and thoroughly. You should aim for at least one minute each time you drink it.

• Try to eat your food instead of eating it alone. What ingredients do you notice? Any Herbal or Herbal Medicines Clear?

• Observe the signal from your body and stop eating when you feel saturated. It does not matter if the food is still on your plate. You can give it to someone else or leave their remains to a homeless shelter.

To Deal with Emotional Eating Disorders:

I would dare say that most of our bad eating habits are related to emotional problems - sometimes small things like stress or eating at ease, sometimes deeper (but common) problems like food assimilation or food use to handle depression,

To be honest, I had many of these problems when I started about six years ago, deliberately eating, and I still have some stubborn issues.

I ate many emotional reasons: stress, to reward myself for hard work to make a bad day comfort myself when I was sad or alone to prevent problems because others did so, so it was the order and more.

The result was that I grew up in poor health of more than 30 kg and that the hardest time had to change my eating habits. I made several diets (Atkins, flat stomach diets, South Beach), and none of them got stuck because I couldn't understand why I continued to eat things I knew were unhealthy to me. My diet was out of hand.

Only when I began to eat in full consciousness did I realize why I ate so much and why it was so difficult to change. I began to realize how much food was a stool for me and how I used it to handle so many emotions.

Awareness was the beginning. When I realized what happened, the following challenge changed. It is not always easy, because they are habits that have evolved over the years and that we use to meet very real needs. Stress is real - if you go with food to deal with stress? How do you handle these needs?

To beat emotional eating you will learn much healthier feelings. I will give you a process that can be used for any emotional dining and some examples.

To Deal with Emotional Eating:

This process is what I recommend to everyone - though you think you do not have emotional eating disorders, you should think because you may have some of the problems that undermine your attempts to eat healthily are unknown.

1.Learn to eat a conscious month. Be aware of your feelings when you think of food (maybe you are hungry or want to eat something). When food and your feelings. Take notes - what feelings do you feel when and why? How do you feel when you eat? You do not need many notes, but you have to make a list of emotions (stress, anger, sadness, joy).

2.First, select a feeling. You may think you can handle more than one. Most people can't.
Therefore, I advise you to start with a first. You get to the next fast. I recommend starting with the emotional triggers that occur most often. So if you have only activated social food only once or twice a week, but have stress or self-timer comfort several times a day, choose it.

3.Search to handle needs in a healthy way. If you need to deal with stress, find a healthy way to do something other than food. If you do not, the need is so great that you give and eat.

4.Pay special attention to your relaxation. If you focus on stress, be aware. Try to notice each time it appears. You can place a visual reminder at a point where you see when you are stressed (e.g. on your desk or in the car if it is where you often feel stressed).

5.Contact the new healthy handling techniques when the trigger occurs. If the technology goes a step further with stress, take a walk every time you experience relaxation, even if it only takes one to two minutes. If you want to eat desperately, use the new addressing technique.

6.Call the right social support. Ask your friends and people online to support your new change.
Daily reports with them and asks them to hold you accountable.

This is not a comprehensive list, but some examples of how to meet your needs without food. During the experiment, you may find other better ways for you. The key is to start!

Stop Obsessing About Food and Emotional Eating:

Hunger for love is much harder to eliminate than hunger for bread.
- Mother Teresa

When you reach the point where you can no longer do it, it's time to change the situation. The obsession with food and emotional nutrition cannot be further tolerated.

You know, emotional eating is more than calming fear. You still have one thing to do to live your life in peace, fulfillment, and good health.

If you follow the steps below, you are well on your way to becoming a conscious ether, and eating emotionally is a past.

Recognizing the body's needs is a way to better understand you. You learn more about your needs and experience the best way to meet them. You learn to know your limits and the possibilities of your life. First and foremost, you learn what you need to take better care of yourself.

1. Eat When You Are Hungry

Courage is a kind of salvation. - Plato

I know it sounds like a complete simplification, but how often do you refuse to eat? Do not eat anything or eat certain foods.
When your body needs food to get energy, there is simply no substitute for food. They can distract themselves and postpone the meal for so long.

Your game signals remain silent for a moment, but you can rest assured that they will return and you cannot ignore them!

Eat a balanced meal. It's great if you're looking for a balanced meal or snack because you meet both needs at the same time!

Enjoy Your Food:

Choose wisely what you eat to get both the physical nourishment your body needs and the satisfaction that your mind and heart need.

Sometimes you only eat fuel. We live all hectic lives and sometimes eat is just one way to reach a goal: put more fuel in the engine so you can continue.

Eating is also an important way to enjoy life. If you don't like what you eat at a certain level, you will remain dissatisfied and dissatisfied most of the time. This leads to an obsession with food and emotional food. Eat at least once a day to revive and enjoy the fun.

2. **Be Present:**

The Point of Power is always present. -Louise L. Hay

Only do one thing while eating.

If you're driving, watching TV, working on your computer, playing a game on your iPad, reading, etc., you can't really know what you're eating if you like it if you're hungry for food if you have enough etc.

Distraction is a way to solve feelings of guilt or shame about what you eat, how you eat it, how you think about yourself and your body.

Derived food can be more about your relationship with yourself, your need for compassion and your need for food.

Mindful Food is a tool that you can now use to enjoy taste, texture, aroma, color, etc.

If you eat wisely, you will be able to judge your relationship with food and how you respect your body. The good thing is that it also prevents you from being obsessed with food and emotional food!

3. Determine Your Feelings:

The best results always pass. Robert Frost

Assure the fear of food instead of eating to relieve fear. Easy to say, right?

This can be difficult because hunger is getting worse. Anxiety can also be one of the first signs of hunger. It has become very complex. Our ancestors had to search for food, maybe they were a little worried, and when they had time, they found it and ate it. Although there is plenty of food today, if you ignore hunger, you may feel very nervous.

Help slowly. Do the best tricks, reduce anxiety, take a deep breath, some quiet yoga, short-term meditation, about 2 to 5 minutes, then a balanced meal or snack. The food will wait.

Anxiety is one of the most common emotions that lead to an emotional diet. Eating something can be done, distracting the problem, and depending on the food, your mind is stimulated to release soothing chemicals from the brain.

The solution is to identify the problem and find out why and do everything possible to correct the situation.

Sometimes this means that you have to develop an action plan, and sometimes you do everything possible, quiet and quiet.

Improve your understanding of the emotions you feel most often. Emotional awareness is your personal guide to preventing emotional diets.

If you know what will happen, you have the opportunity to take care of yourself. Emotional eating is no longer a distraction that really disrupts your things. You know, you can choose how to deal with yourself.

4. **Ignore the Ethical Choice of Food:**

Maintaining a healthy relationship with food means that you are morally unfit or deprived of your dietary habits. - Evelyn Tripol
Eating is not a sin! How many delicious foods?

How many times have you heard them, usually with candy: "Are we tonight too bad?" What if we accepted an enjoyable experience with our bodies, such as food?
True acceptance means satisfying your desire for a pleasant experience with worthless food.

If you accept the fact that you are a favorite Easter, you can accept time, and if you eat only as fuel, know that you will eat more comfortably soon.

Sometimes we just need to eat and cheer. They have a great

meeting. 14. It is important to have a balanced lunch in the afternoon.

Sometimes you only eat for happiness. Think of a Christmas cake or special food that you use only at holiday parties. These foods and rites that you eat symbolize the importance of the present.

Food has a different nutritional value and has no other moral value. Eat well and enjoy.

5. Search for New Contacts:

Love is not what we give or accept, it is what we keep and develop, only the links between two people can be preserved - we cannot love others like us. Brian Brown

An emotional diet can be motivated to reunite a person, memory, thoughts, emotions, etc.

If you want a particular food, they are the memory or the person you want to contact, nutrition is a way to do it.

Emotional eating is the way you want to experience relationships. The problem is that an emotional diet cannot help you connect the way you want, or communicate with others or yourself.

By educating your emotional food and the emotions it brings you, you can focus on what you need. Awareness can help you focus on your obsession with food relationships and meet your needs.

Through these five simple things, you do a lot of things, so you have to stop eating emotionally, and you can never follow a diet. You have the answer you need. I hope some of the tools listed above can help you find them!

Conquer Emotional Eating With These Weird Tricks:

Your mind has been kidnapped! They are blindfolded only, with sweet and fragile chocolate mouths. For some time, gives you a sense of satisfaction, reconciliation and other wonderful feelings. But then she blamed it: "I did it again, where is my will?" You are not hungry, how did this happen? You cannot control your likes. Can you take another choice next time? Of course, you can continue to learn.

An emotional diet can begin in childhood, when your diet becomes one of the favorite recreational treatments for your parents in response to your emotions and behaviors. As a child, empty your cries with a bottle. When they were young, they used sweets, snacks, ice cream and various desserts to reward their good behavior. As an adult, you can eat junk food because it reminds you of childhood memories.

Holidays and special events are always about food. There, eat too much to celebrate the joy of the concert, and enjoy it fully and "out of the house." Or use food to soothe and distract your attention, relieve pain and relieve tension. Meeting is full of family.

Eating can also be a way to destroy you unconsciously. Protecting your identity and belief system depends on your mind. If reality is not what you want, your mind will make every effort to resolve this contradiction. If you start to lose weight and with the arrival of the diet, you think you are fat and not worth, guess what? You will fall into self destruction and over-eating. Your subconscious mind helps to unify your reality and yourself image. To interpret it differently, imagine your mind as a heat. When the thermostat is set, the heater or air conditioner is turned on to adjust the temperature accordingly, and the temperature is maintained indefinitely. When your mental "thermostat" is 170 lbs down to 135 lbs, the thermostat of your brain will restore self- destruction and restore you to the weight you imagine / expect.

Food can be a mechanism to adapt to wounds. Excess fat can be the physical representation of the emotional shield that builds around you. If you get rid of it, you may feel weak and weak. So you can rebuild it again.

Our subconscious strength is used by the food marketing industry. Their perfect taste and smell and the touch of food make us addicted. Food is not about food, but about dealing. "When you're hungry, you're not yourself," Snickers said. IHOP promised, "Come hungry, happy." "Every dinner must be very delicious," Stoffer said. Who among us does not want to build our "lunch with Arius"? The list is still going on. It creeps. (The best-selling salt fats are a great review of US food companies that use mood foods.) Whether you are eating emotionally or not, read 12 tips to help you control your emotions and overcome your emotional diet.

1. **Tell Yourself to Change the Story:**

Talk to you all day long. Not strong, but in your mind. This sound will not stop! We have analyzed, criticized, minimized and explained. If you tell yourself that the bad story is "I feel bad if I do not eat snacks", replace it with something stronger. "I'm proud of taking care of my body and refusing unhealthy snacks!" Consciously decide to change the story that tells yourself that it will change your interpretation of the brain and create positive feelings. Certainly will fight the negative emotions caused by old stories. This requires practice, so do not give up if you return to a negative internal letter! Jump in the car again. For those involved in psychology, this technique may be a framework called Cognitive Behavioral Therapy or Cognitive Behavioral Therapy.

If you still hear that your internal critics are claiming that you are "fat" or laughing at your appearance, try this exercise: first tell the internal critic "Thank you for sharing" and then close your eyes before saying anything positive. Ask for more fun and add your inner voice. Repeat this process until you no longer hear this internal passive speech. In short, you are trying to control the unpleasant internal criticism you do not like.

2. **Change Your Reward System:**

Disconnect food from the rewards system and begin rewarding yourself with other satisfactory activities. For example, you can walk or shop on your wish list or enjoy a massage or a hot tub.

3. **Changing Your Mind is the Key to Changing Your Body:**

NLP is a powerful system for reprogramming thinking. Try NLP to communicate with your favorite snacks: Close your eyes first. Think of the favorite food you want to avoid. For example, you may not stop eating pizza? Now think about the things that make you scared. Suppose you are spoiled by spiders and cockroaches. Imagine the delicious pizza you love so much. Spiders and clams emerge from steamed cheese. The more you realize that this realistic "video" is in your mind, the more realistic and cumbersome, the harder it is if you want the pizza you dream of.

4. **Enjoy Yourself as if You Were a Glorious Little Kid:**

We do not treat strangers or even respectable children because we treat ourselves. Have you criticized some stupid things? Did you say that you are useless? For all holy things, please offer love, respect and good faith! Protecting the emotional essence is your task. The feeling of safety, strength and protection will lead to an emotional diet.

5. Develop Small Habits Successfully:

Develop new licensing habits, such as regular training or record your small achievements when you reach your goals. This triggers your mind to endorphins, so you should stay in good shape and stay healthy.

6. Keep Your Commitment to Yourself:

You practice by keeping your promises and achieving the goals that lead you to a healthier life. If you are used to keeping your promises, you are motivated and motivated from within.

7. Do Not Keep Garbage at Home:

Life is easier with fewer temptations. Did you know that the will is a definitive help and will decrease during the day? Packaging a jar of cookies will waste your will so you can work on important life goals. Don't target cookies because your brain knows they are always present. Throw the cakes instead - like throwing them in the bin! You save a lot of willpower. Instead of keeping snacks for yourself, you can fill your fridge and pantry with healthy settings (mini carrots, do you mind?).

8. Create a New Identity:

Make an alter ego or an avatar, a new version 2.0 of yourself with the characteristics of the person you want to become. Imagine this new powerful, happy and safe version of yourself that you can easily handle different emotions without having to run in the fridge. Adopting a new, healthier and stronger identity can change many disturbing behaviors, not just overeating.

9. Reduce Stress:

The diet is stressful. The search for someone else, whether it be a celebrity on television or a friend who sent a bikini photo by itself on Facebook. Trying to be someone else can drive you crazy. Today, there is a lot of pressure that we have a certain angle, especially for women. If you are the type of person who suppresses this pressure and overcomes emotionally, you must reduce stress. Try relaxation techniques like mindfulness meditation, yoga or just relaxing by the pool. Watch a funny movie. Laughter is really the best medicine. Stress triggers junk food cravings and releases the hormone cortical, which stores fat in your body! The goal is to be happy and relaxed.

10. Breathing:

Breathing not only relaxes you, it can also release you from negative emotions that make you eat too much. Here's a simple breathing that you can do every time you feel overwhelmed: Sit down in a comfortable position with your eyes closed and your back straight. Place your hand on your stomach, breathe deeply through your nose and slowly breathe through your mouth. Continue for at least 3 to 5 minutes. In this state of relaxation, your desire for junk food falls.

11. Make a Conscious Choice:

For some people, the goal is to make a conscious decision and stick to it. Make a list of all the pros and cons of an emotional diet. By focusing on your goals, you strengthen your willingness to make a lasting change in your life.

12. Change Your Value System:

Determine your state of health based on your immediate satisfaction with evaluating your long and short-term results. Living in a healthy, lean and moving body is more satisfying than the immediate satisfaction you get from eating attacks.

Excessive consumption of unhealthy foods may be due to feelings that are not useful to you. The good news is that you control your emotions. Determine your emotional triggers, watch out for these triggers and take control of your body and mind. Managing your emotions is an acquired skill. You improve with practice. This is reflected in how you feel and how you look. Are you sure you can't wait?

Chapter # 6

Good Food Reduce Mood Disorder

People can change their lifestyles in different ways to control their fears. Foods rich in vegetables, fruits, whole grains, and fat-free proteins may be useful.

Concern spreads and affects millions of people around the world. Symptoms vary, and some people feel them at times. However, people with symptoms may suffer for 6 months or more of generalized anxiety disorder (GAD).

GAD symptoms include mental and physical symptoms such as:

- Fear
- Excitement
- Excessive attention to daily events and issues
- Irritability
- Difficult concentration
- Personal social and professional relationships have problems
- Heart palpitations, heart rate accelerates
- Muscle tension
- Feeling tight chest

Doctors often combine GAD and treatment, including

conversational therapies such as cognitive behavioral therapy (CBT) and medicine. Sometimes these traditional treatments do not work in the long run. However, some studies have shown that adequate nutrition can help improve symptoms.

Eating Good Foods Can Reduce Anxiety:

Brazil Nuts:

Brazil nuts are rich in selenium. Selenium can improve mood by reducing inflammation, which usually increases with mood disorders such as anxiety. Selenium is also an antioxidant that prevents cell damage. It is also carcinogenic and can prevent the development of cancer.

Nuts, animal products and other vegetables such as mushrooms and soybeans are excellent sources of selenium.

It is important not to consume too much selenium because this can cause side effects. The recommended maximum limit for adult selenium is 400 micrograms (μg) daily. days. Be careful not to take large doses of supplements or eat more than three or four Brazilian brazilian daily.

Brazilian nuts and other nuts are good sources of vitamin E. Vitamin E is an antioxidant. Antioxidants can be used to treat anxiety, and some studies have shown that low levels of vitamin E can cause depression in some people.

Fatty Fish:

Bold fish such as salmon, mackerel, sardines, mackerel and squid are rich in omega-3 fatty acids. Omega 3 is a fatty acid closely related to cognitive functions and mental health.

However, recent research has shown that someone is taking a lot of other fatty acids, called Omega-6, which are not enough to increase the risk of emotional disorders due to anxiety. .

Foods containing omega-3 alpha-linolenic acid (ALA) contain two essential fatty acids: Eicosapentaenoic acid (EPA) and docosahexaenoic acid (DHA). EPA and DHA regulate neurotransmitters, reduce inflammation and enhance brain function. A small study of 24 drug abusers found that EPA and DHA supplements reduced anxiety. More research is needed. Current recommendations recommend eating at least two fatty fish a week. A study found that men who ate squid three times a week reduced anxiety.

Salmon and sardines are among the few foods that contain vitamin D.

Vitamin D:

Researchers are increasingly linking vitamin D deficiency to mood disorders such as depression and anxiety. A report published in the Journal of Emotional Disorders found that there is sufficient evidence that vitamin D promotes depression. Other studies in pregnancy and older adults have also shown how vitamin D improves mood. Vitamin D can also improve seasonal disease (SAD) in the winter.

3 Eggs:

Egg yolk is another good source of vitamin D.

Eggs are also a good source of protein. It is a whole protein, which means it contains all the essential amino acids needed for human growth and development.

Egg also contains tryptophan, an amino acid that helps produce serotonin. Serotonin is a neurotransmitter that helps regulate mood, sleep, memory and behavior. Serotonin is also believed to improve brain function and reduce anxiety.

Pumpkin Seeds:

Pumpkin seeds are an excellent source of potassium to regulate the balance of electrolyte and blood pressure. Potassium-rich foods, such as pumpkin seeds or bananas, can relieve symptoms of stress and anxiety. Pumpkin seeds are also a good source of zinc. A study of 100 female students showed that zinc deficiency can have a negative effect on mood. Zinc is important for the development of the brain and nerves. The largest zinc reserves in the body are in brain regions associated with emotions.

Dark Chocolate:

Pieces of dark chocolate stacked. Scientists have found that dark chocolate can help reduce stress. Experts have long suspected that dark chocolate can help reduce stress and anxiety. A 2014 study showed that 40 grams of dark chocolate helped reduce stress on the pupil.

Other studies have generally shown that dark chocolate or cocoa can improve mood. However, many of these studies are observational studies, so results should be interpreted with caution.

Although it is not known how to reduce dark chocolate from stress, it is a rich source of polyphones, especially flavonoids. A study showed that flavonoids can reduce neuritis, cell death in the brain and improve blood flow. Chocolate contains a high proportion of tryptophan, where the body can create neurotransmitters looking for emotions, such as serotonin in the brain.

Dark chocolate is also a good source of magnesium. A diet that contains enough magnesium or supplements can help relieve symptoms of depression. Look for at least 70% dark chocolate. Dark chocolate also contains sugar and fat; a small portion of 1 to 3 grams (grams) is suitable.

Turmeric:

Turmeric is an herb widely used in Indian dishes and Southeast Asia. Turmeric is an active ingredient in turmeric. Curcumin can relieve anxiety by reducing inflammation and oxidative stress, and usually increases people with mood disorders such as anxiety and depression from this mood. A 2015 study showed that Curcumin can ease anxiety in obese adults.

Another study showed that increased Curcumin in the diet also increased DHA levels and decreased anxiety. Turmeric is easy to add to the diet. It has a small taste and is therefore suitable for juices, curry and pans.

Food That Reduce Stress:

Most people find it difficult to balance life and work commitments. But entrepreneurs may find it almost impossible to find a balance. The pressure to do everything can be overwhelming. If this setting is not enabled, this pressure may cause other problems, including high blood pressure and depression.

To make matters worse, stress causes people to make bad choices. Treating junk food may increase your anxiety and increase the harm to your health. But there are some healthy foods that help maintain a balance of tension. By incorporating them into a normal diet, you will be more root and productive. You can even lose some pounds.

Turkey:

Turkey contains tryptophan, an amino acid that increases the production of serotonin and helps reduce stress. Add turkey to omelets in the morning or cut into salad at lunch.

Spinach:

These green vegetables are an excellent source of magnesium, a metal that promotes calm. Spinach is an excellent source of fiber and can boost your energy levels. Choose to eat salad instead of lunch.

Salmon:

These fish are rich in essential omega-3 fatty acids and help increase serotonin production. DHA (docosahexaenoic acid) in omega-3 fatty acids helps nourish the brain and relieve stress hormones. In addition, omega-3 fatty acids can reduce squid inflammation and promote healthy blood circulation, both of which are affected by chronic stress. Enjoy Alaska Wild Salmon three times a week.

Nuts and Seeds:

Nuts and seeds are rich in essential fatty acids Omega-3 and Omega-6, which helps to reduce stress. Nuts are one of the best sources of Omega 3 fatty acids. Cashews and sunflower seeds also contain tryptophan, which increases serotonin production and reduces stress. Eat some nuts in the afternoon.

Oatmeal:

Complex carbohydrates in oats promote serotonin production. Oats contain lots of magnesium and potassium, which has been shown to lower blood pressure. Eat breakfast in a bowl of nuts, cashew nuts and cinnamon to stabilize your blood sugar and make your day calmer.

Citrus Fruits:

Orange, grapefruit and other citrus fruits are good ways to get vitamin C. Studies have shown that they can reduce stress. In addition, vitamin C is a powerful antioxidant that strengthens the immune system. Have a cup of oranges in the afternoon and enjoy a light, nutritious snack.

Sweet Potatoes and Carrots:

Red crops are a good source of fiber and carbohydrates that can help increase serotonin production. In addition, they can maintain their sugar balance because they are a little sweet. Sweet potatoes and carrots are also an excellent source of vitamins and minerals that are good for blood pressure and heart. In the afternoon eat almond butter, carrots or sweet potatoes several times a week.

Asparagus:

I know that these high legs make your perfume full of fun. But it is rich in folic acid, which is essential for cooling. I found steam and then I added power. I also love to be crispy. Eat as much as possible. (Otherwise you can enjoy these delicious recipes.)

Avocado:

These creamy fruits can protect your body from stress. Avocados are rich in glutathione, a substance that specifically prevents intestinal absorption of some fat, leading to oxidative damage. They also contain lutein, beta carotene, vitamin E and folic acid more than any other fruit. The individual parts (about a quarter of bars) also contain many vitamins B. Keep in mind that this may be a fruit in technology, but I use bold. Use a shared control and adds a new flavor to the slices on the sandwich.

Grain:

Grape contains some of the highest antioxidants known as anthocyanins and has many health benefits, including clear cognition. But all berries, including strawberries, berries and blackberries, are rich in vitamin C and have been shown to help relieve stress. German researchers are testing this by asking 120 people to speak and then solve complex mathematical problems. Patients receiving vitamin C therapy had low blood pressure and cortical levels after a drug resistance test. Replace the berries with other fruits in the diet whenever you want. I also love frozen snacks.

Cashews:

I love all the nuts. These snacks are good because they are bright and a little salty and can cure many cravings. For those who are trying to lose weight, their protein and fat composition is so satisfactory that I find it difficult to recommend it for each meal. (However, be careful when eating this size because it is too hot). Cashew is a very good source of zinc: one meal of an ounce contains 11% of the recommended daily allowance. Low zinc levels are associated with anxiety and depression. Because our bodies do not have the ability to store zinc, it is important to eat every day. If you prefer, you can switch to other nuts using cashew nut. Cut a large piece and place it in the chicken pot.

Chamomile Tea:

This is probably one of the most recommended lollipops. I always wanted it because the flowers are beautiful like small daisies. But it has now proved more than ever that it can relieve chamomile. A study at the University of Pennsylvania in 57 completed a chamomile supplement with general anxiety disorder at 8 weeks and found a significant reduction in anxiety. If you drink it in the form of tea, I definitely loved it more - so you can sit in a quiet place before going to bed and enjoy a warm and wonderful feeling, putting a cup of tea in your hand. . Yes, according to the University of Maryland Medical Center, there is evidence that chamomile does not only remove nerves, it also promotes sleep.

Just pour a cup of boiled water over two tablespoons or three tablespoons of dried flowers (you can buy chamomile bags or tea bags in bulk in a healthy food store) and mix them for 10 minutes. Try a drink every night: turn off your TV, computer, phone, and enjoy a quiet day. It's also very cool.

Chocolate:

In addition to delicious health antioxidants, chocolate is placed above the grocery store and has a clear mindset to communicate. A new study by the University of California, San Diego College of Medicine, showed that women with symptoms of depression are more and that men eat more chocolate. Of course, we were all there and cleaned a lot of chocolate after a bad day. But it turns out that the right amount of chocolate makes you feel better.

It should be noted that dark chocolate reduces blood pressure and helps to improve calm. It contains many polyphones and flavones - two of the important antioxidants - of some juices. You can process dark chocolate once a week, with the addition of snacks or snacks while maintaining weight loss. There are always pockets in your pocket.

Garlic:

Like many plants, garlic is full of powerful antioxidants. These chemicals deviate free radicals (destructive cells, causing diseases and granules that promote aging) and can reduce or prevent some damage caused by free radicals over time. Allicin is linked to a brain component and is linked to the fight against heart disease, cancer and colds. Because pressure weakens our immune system, we need friends like garlic to promote it. As long as you throw it in the broth instead of the oil, you can add it generously to all meals.

Grass Feed Beef:

Beef fed by grass is not only better for the planet, but also for humans. It contains more antioxidants - including vitamins C and E and beta carotene - than cattle that feed on grains, free from hormones, antibiotics or other drugs. Although it usually contains less fat, Omega-3 fatty acid increases by about two to four times. The healthy volunteers who feed the feed increased the levels of omega-3 fatty acids in the blood and reduced the omega-6 fatty acids. These changes are associated with a lower risk of various diseases, including cancer, cardiovascular disease Depression and inflammatory diseases. Roast beef is expensive, but it is worth eating from time to time. (If you are passionate about this concept, check out the local sources of cattle you want to share with other cows.)

Green Tea:

Although green tea contains caffeine, it also contains an amino acid called thiamin. Researchers at the University of Illinois say the diet not only prevents specific cancers, but also strengthens the brain and improves mental functioning. Drink 2 cups a day.

Oyster:

Oysters can only be used as an aphrodisiac! It also belongs to this region because it is zinc Godzilla: six oysters, usually served as appetizers in restaurants, containing more than half of the recommended daily allowance for this important metal. I think it is more suitable for conjunction with lemon wedge ice.

Foods That Will Make You Happy Instantly:

Let's see, healthy food seems boring. Of course, they contain the healthy nutrients our body needs, and we can even help to lose weight if we do some training. But where is the pleasure? I'm sure many of us feel more comfortable eating an ice cream or hamburger than a salad. At least we think we would.

The strange truth is that some foods are designed to make our body happy. Another stranger is that they are not just vegetables. It is true that you can eat your feelings of happiness while enjoying the taste. In that sense, we look at the following foods that will make you happy but at the same time healthy and fun!

Salmon:

Salmon and fish are generally an incredible source of nutrition and happiness. This is mainly due to the high concentration of omega-3 fatty acids that can improve your mood and relieve your mild depression. Bold fish such as salmon also contain high levels of vitamin B12, which may be useful for the production of serotonin. It is one of the neurotransmitters that promotes well-being.

No fish fanatic? No problem, just take a few capsules of fish oil for your daily dose of omega-3.

Spinach:

Okay, I know I said I would leave the vegetables, but there's a reason Popeye destroyed everything. Spinach, along with other green leaves, is rich in folic acid, which is known to reduce fatigue and relieve depression. They also contain high levels of magnesium, which is important for maintaining appropriate levels of serotonin. No wonder Popeye used his horn!

Poultry:

Chicken and turkey contain various amino acids that help you maintain your good mood. The first is Tryptophan, which helps with the production of serotonin. However, be careful, excessive care can cause slowness. The other is tyrosine, which helps the body handle stress. It also acts as a building block for Norepinephrine and dopamine, two of the neurotransmitters responsible for controlling your mood.

Milk:

In addition to a host of nutrients, milk can also play an important role in our mood. The first is due to the fact that it contains iodine, which is important for the proper functioning of the thyroid gland. The thyroid gland regulates almost all functions of the body thanks to the hormones it produces, including your state of mind. The second reason is the presence of whey protein in the milk that should relieve anxiety. Do you have milk?

Brazil Nuts:

Brazil nuts, such as milk, can positively affect thyroid function. They are actually rich in selenium, a micronutrient that helps the body function properly and usually only occurs in plants. What is great about selenium is that it should have an almost immediate effect. This makes the nuts perfect for fast energizing.

Chocolate:

There is a reason why you feel so happy and satisfied after this sweet pleasure because of a group of chemicals in chocolate called N-Acyclethanolamine. They stimulate the channels in the brain to release endorphins, chemicals that relieve pain and provide a comfortable feeling. So if you have chocolate, you will feel happy afterwards. This is important because well being is essential to maintaining our cardiovascular system.

Despite the proven health benefits, we do not allow you to inhale as much chocolate as your heart desires. Moderation is the key. Studies have shown that we need less than 7 grams a day, or 2 or 3 small pieces a week. Make sure these endorphins flow, not be crazy.

Peppers:

This may seem absurd, especially for those who do not like spicy food. But believe it or not, hot dishes can make you happy and give you a sense of well-being. All this thanks to a small chemical called capsaicin, which gives warmth to hot peppers. If you eat something spicy, capsaicin binds to pain-relieving receptors in the mouth and nose mucosa. It then informs the brain that it suffers from releasing endorphins. Maybe that's why some people like spicy food?

Honey:

Honey is a sweet treat that is much healthier than sugar. It can also have a positive effect on your mood. It contains kaempferol and quercetin; chemicals that reduce encephalitis and help prevent depression. Honey also has a much lower influence on your blood sugar level, which means you don't have blood sugar

Coconut:

Coconut can be a great way to love because it contains a high percentage of triglycerides. These are fats that enhance your mood and promote brain health. However, be aware how to get your coconut dose - coconut milk and coconuts are pretty unhealthy. Your best option is unsweetened natural coconut or grated coconut pieces.

Pasta:

That's right People, pasta and other foods high in carbohydrates can be good for your health. They call it a comfort food for a reason. Carbohydrates are excellent because they release energy slowly while helping us feel full and satisfied. The noodles are also full of proteins that contain two important amino acids: L-phenylalanine and tryptophan. As we have already learned, they release endorphins that help improve our mood.

It is important to note that whole grains are a much healthier solution when it comes to carbohydrates. So stick to multigrain bread or whole grain bread, brown rice or basmati and whole grain pasta.

Avocados:

Tryptophan is an essential amino acid used by the brain to produce serotonin - the central nervous system, a sensory neurotransmitter abundant in this fruit. Avocados also benefit the skin, hair and nails. We all know that you are good when you are beautiful!

Grain:

Grapefruit, strawberries and strawberries contain nutrients, anthocyanins and anthocyanins, which help reduce depression and stress.

Chickens:

Vitamin B12 in poultry can calm the body.

Chicken and Pasta:

These central thermal fluids, proteins and fibers are known to treat all diseases. It also improves mental state and increases energy. This may explain why it is also used for colds and flu consumption.

Dark Chocolate:

This generous fun is rich in magnesium, which helps to reduce anxiety and soothe muscles. Dark chocolate also contains phenyl ethylene (PEA), a chemical that makes the brain fall in love. PEA promotes the release of endorphins in the brain. That's why you feel happy when you eat chocolate!

Greek Yogurt:

This healthy appearance is full of probiotics that help improve your mood and immune system.

Green Tea:

Although tea is always a soothing drink, green tea is rich in thiamine, known to reduce stress, anxiety and improve mood. Use high-quality Japanese green tea to get the best value for money.

Swiss Beet:

These green vegetables are rich in magnesium and are especially beneficial to women because they help them to better control stress, improve sleep quality and relieve menstrual symptoms.

Tomatoes:

Lycopene - antioxidant in tomatoes - can fight encephalitis. Because lycopene is soluble in fat, tomatoes use a small amount of olive oil to help the body absorb lycopene.

Nut:

Nosh nuts are ideal for improving mental state and rich in B vitamins. These help maintain emotional balance, fight fatigue, anxiety, tension, tension and irritability. In addition, nuts are rich in omega-3 fatty acids that promote good brain function and prevent depression.

Can Food Make People Happy?

They went home after a long day's work. They do not want cooking and do not want to eat on the road. You are so hungry that you do not go home to eat; all you have to do is go to the parking lot to eat burgers or tacos or anything sitting in the driver's seat. Then you feel a bit blocked and fat. You can feel guilty and repressed.

Then there are other times when you take the time to prepare a healthy dinner that you love and enjoy. You will feel saturated after these meals - and very happy.

Is not it odd that the food makes us happy? Finally, we eat to feed ourselves. The food we eat with nutrients such as proteins, fats and carbohydrates, uses the body as fuel and other important tasks. We also get vitamins and other nutrients from food that we cannot eat but still need. Of course, we need food, but why make some foods happy when we eat it?

Discover the science of happiness why some foods make us happy. Some foods appear to contain compounds that affect our mood. The most interesting thing is that avoiding certain foods may have the opposite effect and increases the risk of depression.

In the next few pages, learn about the performance of science in the search for culinary luxury. The first is the food.

To understand how food makes you happy, it is important to understand how your brain regulates your mood. The brain uses neurotransmitters as communication signals to communicate with other parts of the body and release commands "Breathing, heart!" The brain tells when octopamine is sent to the receptors in the nerve fibers that form the myocardial tissue [Source: Johnson et al.].

The same is true for emotional stability. There are two types of neurotransmitters responsible for our emotions: inhibition and excitement. Intense neurotransmitters like Pferraz stimulate the body and mind. But after a long period of pregnancy, we have become fed up with this kind of neurotransmitters and may cause dissatisfaction. Neurotransmitters such as serotonin have a calming effect on the brain and partly inhibit the action of exciting neurotransmitters. Finally, if there is a balance between the two, there is an ideal mentality.

However, these chemicals that change the mood have not fully recovered. They are produced by compounds in food, and some foods support neurotransmitters better than others. We call this food happy.

In general, most serotonin neurotransmitters are well connected because they need to regulate sleep and pain. It is also a powerful source of control for exciting neurotransmitters [Source: Neuroscience].

The foods that support the production of serotonin are spinach, turkeys and bananas. Spinach contains high levels of folic acid, a vitamin B used to produce serotonin. Bananas and turkeys contain high levels of tryptophan, an amino acid that is converted into serotonin in the brain. Tryptophan enters the brain directly through the barrier of the protective cell between the blood stream and the brain. This makes tryptophan very rare because serotonin cannot cross the blood barrier in the brain [Source: Hyde and Jengenbach].

Another important neurotransmitter that helps to regulate and stabilize the mood is gamma aminobric acid (GABA), known as natural stability, because it has a calming effect on the body. GABA is produced during the Krebs cycle, a physiological process in which food is converted into energy for cell use. Food does not contain GABA, but some contain neurotransmitter components, an amino acid called L-glutamine. Pork, beef, sesame and sunflower seeds contain high concentrations of glutamine [Source: Nerve Composition]. Because L-glutamine can also cross the blood barrier in the brain and support GABA production during the Krebs cycle, these foods can have an indirect but beneficial effect on your happiness.

Although some foods contain mood swings, some foods make us feel comfortable eating them.

There is a big difference between foods containing compounds that affect the chemistry of the brain and food, which makes us feel comfortable. The last group of food is called rest food. While forming a happy body of food can affect our physiology, comfortable food can be fun, but if you're in a landfill, as long as you feel better, the difference may not be important to you.

Psychological research shows that the preparations we want to prepare are actually antiques to our past [Source: Gallison]. We all have memories of happy times, as eating reminds us of those moments, we consume the symbol of the happiness of the past.

Comfortable foods may also be associated with some people in our lives: Eating a particular food that someone loves can create a happy idea by releasing memories or associations of that good person. [Source: Wansink] This allows everyone to enjoy unique calming food. If your birthday is a happy world for you, if you are blue, you may have a birthday cake or a candy change.

Although welfare food (or related events) varies from person to person, the foods that we associate with soothing or happy feelings vary by sex. A study by Cornell University of 277 men and women in 2005 showed that women tend to rest with sweet and sugary foods such as ice cream, while men prefer comfortable foods such as steaks and soups. [Source: Smith]. The study also showed that men may use cooked dishes as rewards, while women often feel guilty.

It should be noted that women's errors may refer to evolutionary considerations for males. An enjoyable and stressful diet that adapts to stress - especially chronic stress - is unhealthy behavior similar to smoking. A 2007 study showed that participants ate more popcorn while eating raisins and popcorn butter while watching a sad film [Source: Lang].

Happiness has proven that food can make you happy. The absence of certain foods - or at least some of its essential ingredients - will make you really sad. Fatty acids called ducoshexenic acid (DHA) is the most common fat in the brain. It is good because it is an important part of the structure of the brain. It is also very easy to get. Seafood are two important sources of DHA. A study conducted by the National Institutes of Health (NIH) found a link between DHA deficiency and increased depression in the United States.

Although there is no direct causal relationship, other studies support the relevant links found by NIH. A study found that countries that eat small fish in North America and Europe are 10 times more likely to suffer depression than Taiwan, and Taiwan is one of the most important sources of food for fish [Source: Franklin Institute]. Although it is not a reason, eating fish and other foods that contain DHA is a good cause.

It is curious that although some foods have improved mood of the brain, eating restrictions may have a greater impact on happiness. A hormone called lysine enters the brain and tells it is time to eat. When you produce lysine, you are very hungry. Once you have finished eating, the production of ghrelin stops and your brain stops getting hungry.

But if you do not eat anything, the production of the hormone ghrelin will continue, and hormones accumulate in the brain. Although the increase of the ghrelin hormone can prolong hunger, the researchers found that this hormone can also be used as an antidepressant for depression. A 2008 study by the University of Texas showed that rodent-injected rodents showed fewer signs of stress and anxiety [Source: Luther et al.]. Interestingly, low-calorie rodents (40% of normal calories) rodents with the same calorie content had the same result.

It seems that the best way to be happy is to eat nutritious foods that affect brain chemistry, but therapists should sometimes make you happy. A healthy balance between nutrition and soothing foods may help maintain a person's best mood.

Chapter # 7

Change Your Relationship with Food

Do you usually say what you ate causes complex feelings? On the one hand, you really want comfort; on the other hand, you will stick to your structure for healthy eating.

We, humans, have a complex relationship with food, but frankly, this is not our fault. This has nothing to do with the fact that we are not strong enough. Only the flow disappears over time. So, if we want to eat healthier, we cannot rely solely on will. Today we invite coach Manna Stone to learn more about how to build positive relationships with food so we can live a healthier life.

Diet is an Emotional Experience:

Eating is passionate and intimate. As a child, we feed, love and move on at the same time. When we are angry, our breast milk will comfort us. The food was always very touching; let's show the love of others.

Happy husband, I eat breakfast, too, chat, inside, coffee people eat together. Healthy Eating and Reasonable Foods the mission we live in a food company is to create a world of food that has the same effect on us. For this reason, many products add a lot of sugar, which gives us intimacy, so this feeling is often lacking in this world.

How Can Our Food Help Us Get Access To Navigation?

1. Do Not Forget What You Eat:

First of all, we are all grown fruits, vegetables or meat. It is still vivid and generated for our consumption. Most of them have eaten a lot of time and have done a lot of work to put these foods on their plates, no matter where they are. This is something you should be grateful for, all the hands that can bring you food and miracles that are obtained from the ground and prepared for your hands.

Be Aware Of Your Senses:

Secondly, we can focus our attention on our senses. What do you see, feel, taste and even feel? If you're interested in all these things, every part of it might be an adventure. You will notice the new things you have dealt with several times.

Have You Really Tasted It?

If you try the food, something else can happen. According to my experience, most of the empty food you eat loses its attractiveness suddenly. Do not please me as I used to, I no longer want it. I advise you to try this. So if you still like it, you'll find that some bites are usually enough to suppress the urge to smoke.

2. Remember Why You Eat:

There are many reasons why we choose to eat. We can feel tension, boredom, loneliness, or loneliness. I've learned to use these things because "excuses" are wrong, but I tell you that these are very good reasons.

As I said, the diet is emotional and nourished by the body. Emotional eating is normal, we've done it. The problem is that food is our only response mechanism. Our comfort may be great, but it does not solve what is going on.

When I noticed that I wanted to eat for purely emotional reasons, I would like to ask myself the following questions:

- What has already happened? How do I feel? Why?
- How can I help me better now?

If you eat anything, do it! But maybe you call a friend, someone who bothers you, changes. Do we have a situation that is not right for you or something that can help you face it? Consider all options before making a choice.

3. See How You Talk About Food:

The way we talk about food is often frustrating. Because my job is to enable you to make decisions based on self-love, this is an important issue you need to talk about.

If you eat well, you cannot eat anything (except for medical reasons). You never have to say you have nothing. Because who decided? Who are they? No one sees your choice of food except you. From now on, you can eat what you want. It is up to you to take more loving choices at every moment. If not, just say "No, thank you" for your choice.

4. Be Careful When Talking About Your Body:

I would also like to encourage you to talk about your body in a friendly manner. It doesn't matter how it looks. He is worthy of your love and respect. If this is difficult for you, you can follow many inspirational accounts for the body and positive for the body on Instagram. We've learned

to hate every ounce of fat in our body. The only reason this announcement is announced to us is that it is a market. People can make money with uncertainty. It will be much more difficult if we choose to love ourselves. Does the body mean positive that we stop eating healthy? Not at all, but healthy and thin are not the same. In many places on the scales, we can be happy and healthy.

Think about what and why you eat and how you talk about food and your body so you can build a more loving relationship with food.

Improve Your Health Through Relationships With Food:

For those of us who have high demands on time, the daily diet will often have no time to rush to enjoy or even enjoy the food we eat. It seems that the relationship with the food we eat is unconventional, but it is actually necessary to maintain a healthy balance in our bodies. The principle of "full-consciousness diet" is rooted in the teachings of Buddhism and remains part of the current concept of physical and spiritual harmony. This seems to be an abuse of time, but it may be closer to reason, physical and spiritual enlightenment, but while enjoying the taste of each of our foods while reducing our diet.

"A conscious diet is a technique that anyone can use to educate people about what to eat and how to eat it," said Daniel Hart, editor of Daily News. "Although this has become commonplace recently, not all anger loses weight, but it is about increasing awareness of diet and diet, but you can understand the needs of hunger and energy in your body more effectively because you can prevent you eat too much."

To understand a conscious diet, we must first examine the concept of mind. According to the American Psychological Association, "attention" refers to a state of mental awareness. The rational mind can be achieved through a variety of exercises, including meditation, yoga, tai chi and healthy eating. While attention seems to be a holistic approach to physical and mental health, many experts are aware of these benefits. Awareness is a useful technique for reducing stress and improving cognitive skills and emotional satisfaction.

The Daydream Center identifies the principles and values of a healthy diet and the goals that people who use them can achieve. First of all, you should focus your senses on the food in front of you. Take a moment to look at your meals (texture and color) and think about what to prepare. To do this, we must eliminate all external interference, including our smart phones, our televisions, and more. Then take a spoon full of everything you want, but do not eat it anymore. Just think that you should eat food instead of actually eating it. You may think that food expectations have given you a new understanding of the relationship between foods.

"Many of us eat in an environment that distracts you-you can drive or run TV, or you can have breakfast or lunch in your office," Hart said. "When you choose food, you cannot listen to your inner wisdom and tell you what kind of food will bring you a good, healthy and healthy feeling. You can eat things faster and easier, or eat with your friends. Eat with your food, and you do not know what to make you feel. "

When it comes to finally eat, do not confuse everything on the dish and eat heavily. Taste each ingredient of your dish to understand the ingredients of the meal. Place a spoon or fork between each mouth and take some time to enjoy your taste. I feel cracks in the food and avoid swallowing very quickly. Be aware of your feelings to fill with every bite, and do not be afraid to pay attention to what you love and what may be boring. Talk about it, what kind of food you eat is unimportant. Everything from fried chicken to salad can be eaten carefully.

Remember: your senses are the best weapon you can eat. Strengthen these senses by focusing on your meal and swallowing whatever may catch your eye. By eating, you can feel full without eating normal amounts. This is the reason for the exercise. Realize that your relationship with the body is to know when we are full and when to eat too much.

Change Your Relationship with Food and Overhaul Your Diet—for Good: "Diet" is the four characters that nutritionists and nutritionists hate because they contain only one thing: retreat. We all know the difficulties. Remember, have you promised to remove all the sugar processor and remember your first child, Stevia? Or do you have violence that accuses you of power and the word "naked" is engraved on your arm?

Well, maybe you did not have this before, but most of us think we're poor now. They never work. "Stress is a problem for banks," said nutrition expert / TRENTO Kelly LeVeque. With this in mind, we and LeVeque studied how to build a healthy relationship with the rest of the food.

Read on to learn how you can completely change your diet within 30 days? And how can you change your relationship with food primarily?

1. The Difference between Hunger and Apartment:

Self-esteem is the first step towards greater change. "Some people make informed decisions about food because they think they are healthy and others make decisions about food because they feel good or get used to it," Levick said.

How do we define our habits? "If you decide to eat for three days in a row, it's dangerous, it's like Pavlov's dog, and it's hard to break it," he said.

If you develop bad eating habits along the way, do not blame your will. Levek says that this is also a mistake of your mind. It is the reward hormone that will let you start over and repeat this habit. "

"Your brain needs dopamine, but not very much, and what happens in the end is the regulation of receptors in the brain." "For example, your mind turns dopamine into the cake every day at 3 pm finally, your mind tells you that we have a lot to" regulate one of the receptors - now as human beings, you can get the cookies. "Protein gets the same content as dopamine like dopamine.

2. **Stop Using Food as a Return:**

Habits are not the only reason why we are caught in unhealthy food circles. "It's also about your youth," says LeVeque. "My little sisters and I left the church - because we were damaged - and got a facial slur pie, it was like," It was so boring and terrible; here's your reward for you to start! "It was my childhood!" in the suburbs: you've experienced something boring, here's a reward you've done something good, it's a reward it's your birthday, here's your cake, it's part of our culture to celebrate, but I think it is always important to ask who I am celebrating. Is it your birthday? Did you score the goal? Is it something you should celebrate every week? "

3. **Replace for Removal:**

Once you have understood food and emotional habits, it is time to nourish barter. "If you steal completely, you will bite, so you will think about how I can get the things I like in a healthier version?" Make new habits at four o'clock to replace your old tea instead of a cup of coffee. "If you do enough, you come to a point where you love it more than your previous habit," she adds.

Do you want to fight? "I'm obsessed with my smoothie formula because I think we can give it a taste," she says. "I have a blueberry muffin, so if anyone is used to going to Starbucks for a blueberry muffin and a latte, I ask him:" Okay, how do we do that in the house? "Maybe we get coffee and almond milk, and you make a smoothie that contains proteins, fats and fibers instead of sugar and carbohydrates."

Steps To Rebuild Your Relationship with Food:

For most of my youth, I was unable to control my food and weight. My body did not respond as I thought. I was crazy and found that I was trying to try out all the local dietitians as if they were doing some kind of general exercise.

In the past, I now realize the troubled and negative relationship between me and my body. I hate that. If you struggle and feel hopeless, your body will not be able to meet your needs. Your body will absorb all negative jokes and doubts about yourself and show them under stress. They do not work optimally under stress and pain

In recent years, I have tried my best to relieve negative feelings about food and weight. When I think of a negative idea, these are some of the rules I use.

1. Stop Punishing What I Ate Yesterday:

They will not serve you or your body! In fact, your body will hear this negative disease that causes undue pressure on your body! Stress is the leading cause of health death.

2. Responsible for Eating and Drinking:

In fact, please see. Try it and feel it. Use your senses! Enjoy album content. In this way, your mind sends a "satisfaction" signal, and they are less likely to eat too much.

3. Thank You for Your Food!

I hate to look like another health minister, but gratitude can change your life. This gift: feed your body in good faith. Your heart, hormones, brain and cells need nutrition to work for you.

4. Enjoy the Food;

Do not confuse the eating experience with negative thoughts such as "I should not eat this" or "If I cannot control what I eat, I'm wrong." Your body will show these thoughts under physical pressure! Find out if you have better digestion! Get along with your board and live in peace.

5. Stop the Vicious Circle of Everything or Anything:

If you decide to eat a bad meal, try to leave it! Your body will listen to what you usually do, not at times! Most of us think, "Well, I've eaten this donut, so I can continue." Now you can see where the problem occurred. Your body does not care about a lot of cakes, but when you fill your stomach, you'll start taking care of the rest. He just does not know how to handle everything.

6. Practice Positive Affirmations:

Confirmations are a powerful tool for turning negative thoughts and reprogramming your beliefs, behaviors, and actions. They can change the way you see the world and have certainly helped me improve my relationship with my body. I like some

This plate of food is so good to me. My body knows how to use this food.
My cells no longer get so much kindness.

7. Give Up on the Need to be perfect and eat:

I promise no one will eat perfectly. Not me! The perfect does not exist! Try to drop that need and remember that you are good enough.

8. Stop Comparing!

Your body and your nutritional needs are different from your friends, your sister and your mother! Your relationship with food has nothing to do with you. They have a completely separate and complex body mechanism. They can't take their relationship with their food personally, dear!

9. Don't Be So Hard With Food:

It is important that your healthy lifestyle does not affect your social life. (I try very hard for that!) If you are traveling with family and friends, don't worry about eating places. It does not matter. Simply select the best one that is available to you. Otherwise, you only complicate your relationship with the food.

10. When You Eat When You Are Not Hungry, Something Happens Emotionally:

I invite you to stop and ask yourself what it might be. Why are you looking for this comfort? Just identify it. If you do not find yourself hungry, I encourage you to do something else that is fun!

Take a walk, massage, swim, paint your nails, meet your partner so you can watch your favorite program with a coffee, talk to your animal or find a variety of health blogs and write your recipes as a favorite! Something!

11. Remember that is all. A life, a body! Enjoy it. Take care of yourself:

Feed him because he needs nutrients. Your body counts on your love and ensures that it works and continues to perform all its biochemical actions! It seems so hard !! I think it deserves our respect. I see my body as my baby.

Love your body; it can't wait to love you!

Chapter # 8

Mindful Eating Helps to Weight Loss

Mind, bring your consciousness to the current practice is the last buzzword of the welfare society
- there are good reasons. Attention cannot enhance empathy, sleep better and reduce stress, but also improves the relationship with food.

This is true - mindful eating is a real exercise that can help shape your body and your nutritional philosophy.

Read on to learn how to use your mindset to choose healthy foods, lose weight and enjoy your meal - no need for error or self-evaluation.

What is Mindful eating?

According to Christa Heinz, deliberate eating, sometimes called an intuitive diet, involves appearances in meals. It's about attracting your attention and focusing on your taste, smell, appearance and sensibility.

Dr Josh Cloppo, a clinical psychologist and a participant in The Web, said that thinking about healthy foods "realizes that the diet is very complex and very sick."

Compare Klapow deliberately with mindful eating: "It's not a matter of spending a little time watching flowers or natural experiences," he said. "We can review it through a temporary assessment, or we can spend a few minutes understanding the entire environment." Mindful eating is exactly the same. "

Can Mindful eating Help You Lose Weight?

"Awareness is not a cure for weight loss, but as part of a method or tool, it can lead to a healthy weight loss diet," Klapow said.

In fact, it is important to choose healthy and nutritious foods to understand body food. According to Heinz, the deliberate diet focuses on the sense of calories and specific foods. "You begin to understand how food provides energy and food for negative events without happiness," she added.

Reducing distraction can also have a big impact on what you eat and how much. If you're distracted, you can notice, make bad choices, and ignore signs of physical discomfort or feeling full.

PaigeBenté, MS, RD, CSSD says that mindful eating can help eliminate these disorders and allow you to adapt better to your body. "It can help you build healthy relationships with food, lose weight, and avoid cycles of deprivation," she said.

Tips to Help You Eat Smarter:

1. **Take a Break Before Eating and Ask Why You Want to Eat:**

An important part of mindful eating understands why you eat. Before eating salsa or fried potatoes at lunch, take a moment to see how your body feels.

Does your stomach look good? Do you feel dizzy or tired? Do you thirsty also consider your environment. Do you feel bored? Do you want to postpone your work?

"Because we eat too much without consciousness, we can eat better in comfort," Klapow said.

2. **Pack Thoroughly Every Bite and Try it:**

Before you close your eyes, remember that in some cases you will drink, peel or breathe accidentally due to extreme hunger or bad habits.

Heinz says this not only prevents proper digestion (and may scare your guests), but it also means that you will lose complex texture and taste of food.

However, if you chew it well, you will notice any salty, sour or sweet taste in the mouth, so you can enjoy the food better.

"With [chewing] you can get more benefits while slowing the recovery process," Klapow said. Instead, concentrate on the small piece and chew it thoroughly before stopping it.

3. **Drink Water Before Meals:**

Preliminary studies have shown that drinking water before meals can prevent over-eating (do not forget to replenish water), but simple rites also have the ability to get rid of independent driving mode and push you to the present.

"This can prevent spontaneous blood circulation from eating by slowing down before eating, so you can focus on the food processor in the future," Kalapov said.

4. **Eat Lively and Aromatic:**

Choose the right food to prepare freshly prepared meals and snacks. By learning to recognize the gentle taste of food while slowing down and eating small foods consciously, you can taste and understand the whole healthy food.

"This will eventually lead to the choice of islands for natural sweetness instead of desserts or vegetables because you like flavor instead of drowning in spices or cheese," Haines said.

5. **Do Not Get Upset When You Eat:**

Turn off the laptop, turn off the TV, and leave the desk. Consciously eating means just focus on eating for you, not through the latest email episodes or magazines or new girls.

Even listening to music or podcasts can be worrisome. Studies have shown that noise from food when eating can have a major impact on eating. This "tight effect" means that if you know the sound that comes out while you eat, you may eat less. But if you cover this sound with headphones, you can use more.

"Imagine it as a meditation," he said. "When people talk to you or stand in front of you or when your thoughts disappear, it's hard to think."

Similarly, when your attention spreads, it is hard to eat healthily - eat notes and signs of body saturation. Consistent study: A derived diet can lead to over-eating, and a strict diet can help you lose weight.

6. Wait A Few Seconds before Waiting:

It takes your mind about 20 minutes to get the full signal of your stomach. It's easy to eat a lot at this small time. So, it's good to rest before putting the second round of paintings.

During this waiting period, Klapow said that you have time to digest the food you eat, and you can deliberately decide another part instead of going back to the kitchen very much.

7. If You Want To Eat, Eat a Cup Of Tea First:

According to Karlovo, "the desire to eat is often just a desire to satisfy the feeling of mouth." In other words, usually, when you are not really hungry, you're just looking for a ritual to give you something.

Then prepare a cup of tea. Try black tea or green tea made with caffeine, mint or unsweetened hibiscus for a rich smell of fresh lemon tea, ginger and apple juice Rooibos.

The boiling water, soaking the tea and putting it in the suspension usually prevent the glands, Kalapo said.

Mindful eating Can Help You Lose Weight:

A small but growing number of studies have shown that slower and more thoughtful diets can help solve all problems and may prevent some people from getting processed foods and unhealthy options.

This alternative method is called "mind." It depends on the concept of mind in Buddhism, where you fully understand what is happening with you and around you. Techniques of alertness have also been proposed to relieve tension and relieve problems such as high blood pressure and chronic gastrointestinal discomfort.

Intention refers to the color, smell, smell and texture of food. The fabric slowly dislodges from distractions, such as. Learn how to deal with guilt and fear of eating. Horace Fletcher, one of the early 20th century foods, thought chewing food could solve many types of health problems.

The Relationship between Mind And Spirit:

Digestion is a complex series of hormonal signals between the intestine and the nervous system. It seems that the brain needs 20 minutes to detect saturation (fullness). If someone eats fast enough, they may feel good after eating too much instead of eating. There is also reason to believe that food activities such as driving or writing can slow down or stop digestion, such as fighting reaction or flying. If we cannot digest it properly, we may lose the nutritional value of some of the foods we eat.

Binger Treatment:

Some studies have shown that mindful eating strategies can help treat eating disorders and eventually lose weight. Indiana University psychologist Jean Christieler and his colleagues at Duke University conducted research funded by the National Institutes of Health on psychoactive techniques to treat over-eating.

A randomized controlled trial included 150 episodes of bulimia and compared treatment based on psychosocial therapy and controls. Both aggressive treatments reduce sting and depression, but it seems that careful treatment helps people appreciate their food and reduces the trouble of controlling their diet. Those who meditate more (during the meal and throughout the day) can benefit more from the program.

The National Institutes of Health has studied the effectiveness of weight loss and weight loss for Christopher and Ruth Wolfer of Duke University. Various other studies are conducted cautiously throughout the country.

A Well-Equipped Kitchen Kit:

Experts increasingly recommend a more mindful and slower diet and eat more carefully every day or week. Here are some tips (and tips) that you can get started with:

1.Set your kitchen timer to 20 minutes and spend some time eating normally.

2.Try to eat with a non-dominant hand. If you are a right-handed person, place the fork on your left hand when you put food in your mouth.

3.If it does not work properly, please use chopsticks.

4.Eat quietly for five minutes; think about what you need to prepare food, from the sun to the farmers, to the grocery store and the chef.

5.Small bites and cloth.

6.Drag and open the following questions before opening the refrigerator or cabinet: 7. "Am I really hungry?" Do other things like reading or traveling?

Mindful Eating for Weight Loss:

The solution contains two important weight loss tips, such as Pritikin faculty members, such as nutritionist Kimberly Gomer and PhD Coral Arvon teaches culinary cooking at the new course at Pritikin.

Are you not exposed to the symptoms of physical hunger and satiety?

Are you not exposed to the symptoms of physical hunger and satiety? Use the hunger scale to restore contact and note unwanted weight loss.

First, we need to exercise hunger and satiety ("I'm drunk"). Secondly, we must take appropriate action.

If you scratch your head and do not know what we are talking about, you are not the only one.

Many people have not been exposed to the symptoms of hunger and satiety in their bodies, which is not without merit. No matter where we go today - every station, every corner, every office - we are seduced by 40 ounces of soda, hamburgers and staff office cakes. We no longer ask ourselves, "Am I hungry?" "Have you finished?" There are nosh and nosh.

If you've read the Pritikin newsletter now, you may not be crunching around cookies anymore but that's fine. But if you are prepared to eat healthy food before the explosion, you may lose weight instead of losing it.

Therefore, it is very important to remember our warnings about hunger and satiety. We say "learn again" because we were born with these trends. Most infants and young children, of course, eat only when they are hungry, and stop when they are full (insufficient).

Nutritionist Prenikine Kimberly Gomer and other Pritikin specialists have learned from extreme hunger, learn about the body's natural signs and improve the chances of losing weight.

Study Shows, Mindful Eating Can Help Weight Loss:

Eating, choosing, and enjoying food that is not distracted by computers and television may help, according to a study.

In the United States, the plan tells people that they can eat what they want, including their favorite high-calorie staple food. But they should take it carefully, taking into account the pleasure of eating, even if they do not have to eat anything.

"We invite people to eat what they like rather than surrender, but eat them seriously," said Dr Caroline Dunn of the University of North Carolina.

"For example, if one of us takes a lot of calories, we recommend eating one or two, but deliberately eating these two foods give him more pleasure.

"Other studies have shown that the first two bites are the most interesting - eating more safely can save more calories, but there will be no more happiness.

"For example, the Chocolate Center ... we recommend that you take it carefully and deliberately and taste the first snacks."

You do not have to waste food. "We ask them to participate or move them home on another day, or buy them in small quantities," she said.

The address is Eat Smart, which moves more, and takes a lighter 15-week work plan. Dunn and his colleagues tested results by recording 80 people, 42 of whom were immediately involved in the program. The remaining 38 people became the control group to be added.

Program participants lost 1.9 kg on average in 15 weeks. Others want to queue up and want to try other ways to lose weight. They also lost a small amount - 0.3 kg.

"Alertness is aware of your environment now," Dan said. "Mindful eating means deliberate eating, intentional eating, intentional eating, eating without intervention, eating only, watching TV, playing computer games or having other distractions, not eating on our desk.

"We are talking about these aspects, so people no longer eat distracted, eat and eat consciously." "People have increased their vigilance and have already lost weight."

Good ideas also related to how people buy groceries and the decisions they make at restaurants. Do you allow yourself to come from abroad because the food you buy at the supermarket is sold to us? "

No diet was offered to study participants; calorie intake was not invited to the calculation. Each week, they discuss another aspect of food and nutrition. Encourage them to increase physical activity.

Six months later, about 75% of the participants and some of them lost weight. After participating in the program, the results of the control group were comparable.

Although the mindfulness has become commonplace and important for improving health, few studies have helped to lose weight or prevent it.

"The results indicate a positive relationship between mindful eating and weight loss." This study contributes to the literature on vigilance because few studies use rigorous methods to evaluate the effectiveness of the mind. "Work hard to be responsible for your diet."

How to lose fast: 3 Simple Steps Based on Science

There are many ways to lose a lot quickly.

But most of them make you hungry and dissatisfied.

If you do not have an ironic will, hunger will prompt you to abandon those plans.

The plan described here will:

Reduce your appetite significantly. You lose quickly without hunger.

Improve your metabolic health at the same time. Here is a simple 3-step plan to lose weight quickly.

1. Reduce Sugar and Starch:

The most important thing is to reduce sugar and starch (carbohydrates).

If you do, your hunger will go down and you will end up eating far fewer calories. Instead of burning carbohydrates as an energy source, your body begins to eat stored fat.

Another benefit of reducing carbohydrates is that it lowers insulin levels and ensures that your kidneys remove excess sodium and water from the body. This reduces a soft feeling and unnecessary water weight.

It is not uncommon to lose up to 10 pounds (sometimes more) in the first week after this diet, both the weight of body fat and water.

This graph comes from a study comparing low carbohydrate and high fat content in overweight or obese women.

The low-carb group eats while the fatty group is low in calories and hungry.

Cut carbohydrates and you automatically eat fewer calories without feeling hungry. In other words, by reducing carbohydrates, autopilot loses fat.

Removing sugar and starch (carbohydrates) from your diet reduces your appetite, insulin level and allows you to lose weight without feeling hungry.

2. **Eat Proteins, Fats and Vegetables:**

Each of your meals should contain a source of protein, a source of low carbohydrate and low fat vegetables.

If you gather your meals this way, your carbohydrate intake is automatically reduced to the recommended range of 20 to 50 grams per day.

Protein sources:

Meat: beef, chicken, pork, lamb, etc. Seafood: salmon, trout, shrimp, etc.

Eggs: The best are whole eggs with yellow.

The importance of eating lots of protein cannot be overstated.

It has been shown to stimulate the metabolism of 80 to 100 calories a day.

High protein diets can also reduce food needs and coercion by 60%, halve the need for night snacks and give you enough calories to get 441 calories a day - just add protein to your diet.

When it comes to losing weight, protein is the king of nutrients. Low carb vegetables:

- Broccoli
- Cauliflower
- Spinach
- Tomatoes
- Kale
- Brysselkål
- Cabbage
- Swiss chard
- Green salad
- cucumber

Don't be afraid to put your plate with this low carb vegetable. You can eat in bulk without consuming more than 20 to 50 net carbohydrates per day.

A diet based on meat and vegetables contains all the fiber, vitamins and minerals you need for a healthy diet.

Sources of fat:

- olive oil

- coconut oil
- avocado oil
- butter

Eat 2-3 meals a day. If you're hungry in the afternoon, add a fourth meal.

Do not be afraid to eat fat because eating carbohydrates and fat is a recipe for failure, they will feel miserable and give up their plan. Prepare each meal from a source of protein, a source of fat and low-carbohydrate vegetables. This brings you in the range of 20 to 50 grams of carbohydrates and drastically reduces your hunger.

3. Lift 3 Times a Week:

You do not need exercise to lose weight in this plan, but I suggest you do it.

The best option is to go to the gym 3-4 times a week. Make warm-up and lift some weight. If you're new to the gym, please ask the trainer for some tips.
Weight lifting burns a lot of calories and prevents metabolism from slowing down, and this is a common side effect of weight loss.

Studies conducted on low carbohydrate diets suggest that you can even get a little muscle while reducing a lot of body fat.

If weight lifting is not for you, doing some exercise like walking, jogging, running, cycling or swimming is enough.

It is best to do some resistance exercises such as weight lifting. If this is not an option, aerobic exercise is also effective.

You can spend a day off every week and you can eat more carbohydrates. Many people like Saturday.

It is important to stick to healthy sources of carbohydrates such as oatmeal, rice, buckwheat, potatoes, sweet potatoes and fruits. But this day alone is a day of higher carbohydrates - if you start to do more than once a week, you will not see great success in this plan.

If you have to eat a cheat meal and eat something unhealthy, do it on this day.

Please note that you do not have to use carbohydrate meals, but you can promote some fat burning hormones such as leptin and thyroid hormones.

You will gain some weight during the day of recharge, but most are heavy and you will lose it again within 1-2 days.

Although not required, it is perfectly acceptable to eat more carbohydrates a day per week.

How to Lose Weight Naturally and Quickly?

Although dietary supplements and supplements have long claimed to provide fast weight loss, most scientific evidence is not available. However, some scientific strategies can affect weight management.

These strategies include exercise, calorie control, temporary fasting, and reduced dietary carbohydrates.

Scientific research supports the following ways to lose weight:

1. Try to temporarily fast

Intermittent fasting (IF) is a short-term feeding program that eats in a short period of time.

Some studies have shown that short-term intermittent fasting for up to 24 weeks leads to weight loss in people who are obese.

The most common ways of fasting are: Fixed Replacement (ADF): Two meals a day, usually on an unpleasant day. In the modified version, the fixed date uses only 25% to 30% of the body's energy requirements.

5: 2 diet: 2 days a week diet is fast. Consume 500 to 600 calories in days of fasting.

16/8 Method: Fasting for 16 hours, only 8 hours. For most people, the window will be at 8 am between dinner and dinner. Studies have shown that eating for a limited period means that participants consume less calories and lose weight.

It is best to have a healthy diet within a few days, not for fasting, fasting and over-eating.

2. Follow the diet and exercise

If someone wants to lose weight, they should know what to eat and drink every day. The most effective way to do this is to log on to each topic in the log or online food tracking tool.

Researchers estimate that by the end of this year, the number of downloads of health applications will reach 3.7 billion. Among them, nutrition applications and weight loss exercises are the most popular. This is not useless because it is an effective way to manage weight because you can stop exercising and lose weight.

A systematic study of physical activity helps to lose weight. A general study found a positive relationship between weight loss, frequency of food consumption and exercise control. Even a simple device such as a pedometer can be a useful tool for weight loss.

3. Eat healthy

Conscious eating is a movement that allows people to see how and where to eat. Through this sport, people can enjoy food and maintain a healthy weight.

Because most people are very busy, they tend to drive on the road, eat behind the office and in front of the television. As a result, many people barely know the food they eat.

Good food techniques include:

Sit down for dinner, preferably on the table: watch the food and enjoy the experience. Avoid distractions while eating - Do not turn on TV, laptop, or phone.

Eat slowly: Take time to chew and enjoy. This technique helps to lose weight because a person's brain has enough time to realize that it is full of signals, thus preventing over-eating.

Expected food choices: Choose nutritious foods that last for hours rather than minutes.

4. Eat protein for breakfast

The protein can regulate appetite hormones and make people feel good. This is mainly due to the reduction of fungal glyline hormone and an increase in saturated hormones YY, GLP-1 and cholecystokinin.

Youth studies have also shown that the hormonal effects of protein-rich breakfasts can last for hours.

Eggs, oatmeal, nuts, butter, buckwheat, sardines and yogurt are great choices for protein-rich breakfasts.

5. Reduce sugar and refined carbohydrates

Western diets contain more sugars associated with obesity, although sugar in beverages is higher than sugar content in food.

Refined carbohydrates are high-processed foods free of fiber or other nutrients. These include white rice, bread and pasta.

These foods are easily digested and quickly converted to glucose.

Excess glucose enters the bloodstream and leads to the insulin hormone, which promotes fat storage in adipose tissue. This helps to gain weight.

People should trade as much as possible in treatment and sweets to get healthier opportunities. Good food fairs include:

Whole wheat bread and pasta instead of white version Fruit, nuts and seeds instead of sugar
Herbal tea and water are rich in fruit instead of sweet soda Juice instead of juice with water or milk

6. Eat more fiber

Fiber is a vegetable carbohydrate, unlike sugar and starch, not digested in the small intestine. A diet rich in fiber can increase satiety and lead to weight loss.

Foods rich in fiber include:

Whole meal cereals, Whole meal, Whole wheat bread, Oatmeal, Barley, Rye fruits and vegetables Peas, beans and beans Nuts and seeds

Chapter # 9

Significant Question of Mindful Eating

Readers have asked many great questions in recent years: "I love ice cream, can I still eat sweets in full consciousness?" And how can I improve my eating habits? Here are the ten most asked questions for readers and their answers.

"If I consciously eat, what happens to my weight?" Should I lose? "

For many people, the answer is: "Yes, it is likely that you will lose." But above all, I say "it depends". Let me explain it in more detail. If you adopt useless eating habits, you can in no way meet the needs of the body. This may mean that you eat too large portions, which increases your weight. However, if you go on a diet or restrict your intake, you will not get enough calories or nutrients. This may mean that your body struggles to maintain a minimal healthy weight. The reason is that this book focuses on improving your eating habits. When you do this, the weight will usually take care of itself. You will notice that this book does not contain the message "You must lose". It's about being healthy than being thin or losing weight. It may mean that you need to eat more nutrients or take better care of yourself. But weight loss can certainly happen because of a careful diet. If you eat what you need to keep your body functioning without giving too much, your body can adapt to your natural weight. Wondering when your body appeared to be in a healthy place for the last time - in terms of weight, health and general well-being?

"Is" Mindful Eating "a Diet? What's Wrong With a Diet?

You've probably already read many diet books. Although this book talks about eating better and maintaining your weight, you can be relieved that this is not a new "diet", it comes and goes in popularity. Conscious food is radically different. It is not about removing food groups or starving themselves. It's something you do in the long run, not something you turn on and off. Diet contains rules that are made for you. These are external recommendations. Predominantly food is geared to discovering what works for you through your intuitive wisdom. For example, a diet may dictate that you cannot eat sugar. But what happens if you have a birthday and your daughter makes you a birthday cake? A diet developed by a nutrition expert is different from a diet. A nutrition expert will help you develop a balanced menu. It adapts to your body's needs instead of trying to adapt to the rules of a particular diet. Professional help in choosing healthy food is a good idea. Therefore, a diet can have a significant impact on your emotional, mental and physical well-being. Diet can interfere with your ability to clarify your body's messages and responses. The lifestyle related to the diet is like taking a knife and cutting the link, which is the only way your body communicates with your head.

"How does consciousness help me eat better?"

Too much food is done automatically. It may be so routine that you may not even know it. As you begin to pay more attention, you notice insane behavior that you have not noticed before, such as biting your nails. When someone - or even you - focuses your attention on your reflective actions by deliberately practicing, you see it and you can begin to change your behavior. If you do not know that you are chewing on nervousness, you are stuck in this pattern. Awareness can help in different ways:

•Mindfulness teaches you to be less aware of stress. This helps you reduce your emotional eating. Interrupting emotional eating can greatly affect your weight and health.

•Stop eating when you are fuller and eat more realistic portions if you are more suited to your body.

•If you are more aware of this, you automatically stop behavior such as. Picking up or grazing food that will make you unconsciously heavier.

•You notice problematic thoughts and feelings about food and how they affect your eating habits (for example, guilt and uncontrollable appetite).

"How do minds help people with different nutritional problems?"

It slows down your speed, gives you a better understanding of weight and helps you get rid of negative automatic circulation of food. So how do you help people who are shrinking, disorienting or emotional? In fact, a wise-minded system was used to treat a variety of nutritional problems, from being unable to lose weight or overweight to everything in between. There are three main ways to diet consciously to solve food and health-related problems:

•Pay attention to signs that your diet will restore contact with your body. Whether you are suffering from excessive eating or vitality, you will forget your hunger and satiety. Note that the diet will return you to your body hints, so you know when to stop and start eating.

•Be vigilant to manage your emotions better. Sometimes people limit or eat too much to overcome negative emotions. Eating and not eating can distract your attention. If you have a more hygienic style, such as mind breathing and relaxation anxiety, you no longer control your emotions through dining options. Feel your feelings, be as uncomfortable as possible, do not push them away or fill them with food.

•Mind changes the way you think.

Eat too much food, overwork, eat emotionally, and so on. You respond to them. You can hear these thoughts without following these ideas. These are useful tips for changing a variety of eating behaviors.

"How do you know good ideas About Mindfulness Eating?"

My first contact occurred with the word "vigilance" when I was a student exchange in Japan when I was a young man.

I live with a host family in a small town near Osaka. My host family taught me a lot of the things I had at that time, including the value of stillness and being. When I was in Japan, they took me to many historical sites, including Zen Garden in Kyoto. From here, I learned the word "vigilance" for the first time. When we were sitting in the garden, my friends knew this word for me - because one of the things that Zen Garden intends to do is develop a sense of righteousness. Though they describe good ideas in words, I remember doing so very clearly. I moved from the attention of my heart to full attendance and full experience. After that, we went to other cultural places and brought the same reaction. We read about the content of the mind and discussed it. This experience changed my way of life. I've learned how to do it really, not jump into the future or think about the past. The real gift is translated into a specialized student and learns how to listen. This skill is of great value in relationships with friends and customers.

During my high school, I learned a lot about college diet problems and eating disorders. The word "mind" became an indispensable part of my vocabulary. I noticed that I frequently used the words "to eat with customers." I began to describe the meaning of these words in detail. Most people know that the word "conscious" means more conscious - but it is a special kind of awareness. I noticed that the client started to say "I'm in the mood to eat dessert a few days ago." It explains the delicate relationship that many people want to establish with food. The goal is not to correct over-eating or eating a little food. Instead, they learn to eat awareness - to the extent appropriate.

"Is there evidence that mindful can help me?"

Yeah! There have been many important clinical studies and developments over the past two decades. A good start is the vision of the work of Dr. John Kabat Zain (2009). His work is crucial to realizing the concept of mind in medicine. A method was found to study the effects of the mind systematically through clinical research. Alertness has been found to help people deal with various medical problems such as chronic pain, cancer and psoriasis (Bayer 2003; Davidson et al 2003). In light of her success in medical issues, psychologists began to study their use in psychological issues such as anxiety and depression, especially diet. Recent studies have found the following results. Dieting can help you:

•Reduce over-eating and over-eating (Christeler and Wolfer 2011; Bayer et al. 2005; Smith et al 2006).

•Weight loss and reduction of BMI (Tapper et al., 2009; Framson et al., 2009; Dalen et al., 2010; Singh et al., 2008).

•Respond to chronic nutritional problems such as anorexia, bulimia, food reduction and physical anxiety (Proulx 2008; Rawal et al. 2009; Hepworth 2011; Lavender, Jard).

"What is the difference between mindful and good ideas?"

The difference between these two terms can be confusing. Both concepts are connected to your mind. But they have different jobs. The mind depends on the level of your consciousness. Have you left or do you know exactly what happened? Eat a robot every time you eat it? Enjoy a variety of sensory experiences? Mindfulness Your thoughts are what you think - what you think. If you listen to the lecture, will you treat it? Do you think of a lot of things to do when eating? Do your internal critics contain messages about what you should or should not eat?

"Mindfulness means I can eat everything?

Yes, you can eat it all. There is no taboo. This restriction caused a batch. For example, if you say you can no longer eat your favorite fruit, you'll need to know how much you want. IMPORTANT WARNING: Although you can eat what you want, intentional food may not eat you. The more you adjust to what you eat and the more you eat, the more specific you are about what you eat. A lady in one of my studios told me a story about the chip. She loves him. One day, she volunteered to attend a school dinner. After an hour, I put some chips in the bag. She told me how heavy her hands were at the end of her service. Her skin was drenched in oil and she did not remove it. Then I looked at her brand new. Most consumers often find that junk food is not quite attractive. To their surprise, its taste is greasy, artificial and overly processed. Sometimes taste buds become more sensitive to reasonable consumers. I noticed that the tea is very sweet or the cereal is full of sugar. What they said, "Oh, very sweet pastries." In addition,

smart consumers control food ingredients to prevent them from being toxic or unhealthy. They found that their bodies felt unnatural after eating preservatives or other additives. Fill whole grains and fruits and make them feel healthier. Smart consumers still eat delicious foods and fast food, but much less, because small amounts of sweets and fried foods become common. So, if you become more aware, your food taste may change slightly.

"What is the difference between cognitive behavioral therapy and mindfulness?"

There are many similarities between Cognitive Behavioral Therapy (CBT) and Attention. Both can help you improve your eating habits. Cognitive behavioral therapy, an intervention aimed at correcting distorted behavior and mentality, is one of the most effective ways to treat certain eating disorders for many years (Zindel et al., 2001). CBT and vigilance are handled slightly differently. Suppose you have a negative attitude towards food. They said to themselves: "The biscuits make me fat." This is an irrational idea. Through CBT, you think of this thinking as negative thinking and replace it with more positive and sensible ideas, such as B. "Biscuits will not make me fat." Be careful not to replace your mind and try not to lose it. Instead, you will recognize this idea and accept the idea. When you stop fighting against your thoughts, you can make them unresponsive.

"Should I practice a spiritual practice or can Buddhists consciously eat?" The roots of yoga are Buddhism and Oriental meditation. However, it is not necessarily a spiritual practice. A conscious diet and breathing yoga use to soothe and soothe the body. This is technology. Eating in full consciousness allows you to maintain any kind of spiritual background or religion - or not at all. But you will find that good ideas will make you more relaxed and live in harmony with yourself. This in turn can improve your spirit.

Questions that help me to Exercise Mindful Eating:

Before Eating:

Why should I eat now?

Ask yourself why you should eat to help assess whether you eat for reasons other than hunger. This may seem silly, but sometimes it says "Athena, why do you want to eat now?" Help me find out if you are really hungry. I may feel very hungry because I do not have enough protein and lunch, or I need to work hard. But maybe I'm looking for a meal because I feel tense, bored, lonely, tired, sad or angry. If I can now realize that I want to eat for emotional reasons because of hunger, I am more able to slow down and not let my feelings make decisions for me.

What is a voluntary level?

A voluntary assessment is another strategy I will use, usually combined with the first question to determine whether I eat because my body needs food or I eat emotionally. Sometimes I will ask myself, "Are you hungry?" I just said I did not really think about it. A hungry assessment will make it more useful, and I find that when the hunger rate is below 5, other things usually happen. In these cases, I will drink a glass of water and wait a moment to see whether the perceived hunger continues or not.

Is this what I think will be delicious?

I always use this. Thinking about whether I will find something tasty and worthwhile, really helps me make the right decision, especially when it comes to food there. I really do not like to eat something I could have done better, or just disappointing. Take the pre-packaged candy as an example. I know they did not do anything for me, but if there were good things already packed in the concert, I might try to find them without thinking about it. Ask myself, "Do you like this, or do you prefer a glass of wine or something more fun?" This decision usually takes me about one second because I can already handle pre-packaged cookies, but I know that my satisfaction factor will be lost. This makes it easier for me to refuse, and I know that I have more preferred alternatives that I can address later, if I really want to allow me to be unrestricted. You can definitely ask yourself this question about the dessert bowl at work or when unhealthy foods are free or rich. Dunks' Free Donut Day is another great example! Dunkin Donuts munchkin is not something special for me, so why do I get one for free on this particular day? When I really want to get one, I prefer to indulge in homemade cakes at the best local bakery in town.

How do I feel after eating?

I know that many people write food magazines to write down all the foods they eat, but these people often miss important parts of the equation. If you are following food, consider keeping track of what you eat only, but also follow how to make your food choices feel good. Write down the feelings of your body, such as swelling, headaches and stomach pains, but try to identify foods that are emotionally upsetting. For example, is there a particular food that causes you to feel guilty after waking up the next morning, frustrated and chilled after eating? Does eating some food make you declare yourself more than others? Eating fried potatoes and salsa sauce will make you always get a towel, just see everything else crazy? Eating ice cream always makes you feel that you need to compensate by reducing food or exercising the next day? Once you can identify the foods that make you feel less physically and / or emotionally (note that some common patterns may take some time!), It is easier and more cautious to answer "How do I feel after eating?" Food will also be selected.

While Eating:

Is this enough taste for me to continue eating?

When I enjoy the food, I will eat food and I will think about whether the food I eat is really delicious. If this is the case, I will continue to take it because it is likely to be worth it to me. However, if I did not know whether I wanted to continue eating, I would remind myself that there was no harm in not completing or throwing out certain things. I did not find that I wasted my samples or indulged in things I did not like at first. If I eat something and it does not suit me, I will confess it and come forward. Basically, if something starts out less than 1 or 2 times, I know you're likely to stop eating it. This is the first rule!

What is the level of satisfaction with this treatment?

This is another ratio problem! I love these because they once again keep you honest and give you a little more meaning. Of course, I might say "Yes, taste good" or "Yes, it's very satisfactory", but if you classify it as five, I may stop and choose something different, and the satisfaction is higher. Again, because I know that I really love her and take a kind of pleasure is the reason for indulging in my soul, not only because I have already taken a bite, so I have completed it.

After Eating:

Am I full now?

After eating, I tried to slow down and let me eat things. Then I will assess how full I am. If I feel tired or want to get hurt, I need to open the level of discomfort in my pants and neck, I will not continue to eat because of the food there. Remember, it often takes longer for your body to reach the fullness you can really understand, so slow down to taste what you eat, and enjoy the atmosphere and companions wherever you eat.

Hopefully these questions will help some of you to understand the ongoing healthy diet better. Every time I eat, I do not necessarily ask each of these questions, but I usually think of some of them. If one of the questions has more problems with you, then try next time to ask yourself this question in a social food environment. You do not have any expectations for yourself, just try it and see what happens!

Remember, a mind diet is a time consuming exercise. Being able to ask these questions myself does not happen to me overnight. It took me many years of practice, and I can honestly say that I would never be perfect. This is a long journey of life, but now when I have slips and weaknesses, I am more able to deal with them next time. I am always the fairest and adjust what is useful to me, but I can only slow down and realize what I feel before, during and after dinner, which is very useful to me! That's why I do not hit myself after indulgence; it helps me move around in the middle, not black and white in everything, which helps keep me sensible!

Questions to Ask Yourself Before You Eat Anything:

If you ever hear words like "deliberate eating" or "eating consciously," you may want to know what it means, or more importantly, how you can exercise it.

As a qualified health professional, I am often asked how to eat more slowly and eat more carefully. So, you develop the following four questions, you should ask yourself before eating.

1. What do I eat?

This is not a superficial problem! Saying "I eat Twinkie" is not enough. You need to know what is in the Twinkie. If you want to know what you eat, then you really need to think about the answer. If you eat something you cannot pronounce, you may not have to eat it. Therefore, reading food labels is very important.

2. Where do you come from?

Does your meal come from a farmer who likes to harvest, or is he from a man wearing a chemical suit putting him in a vicious circle? If you agree that your food contains some energy, you should think about it. Although you do not represent this particular mentality, it is always wise to know the answer to this question. Farmers' food is likely to be healthier than factory food. Do not believe me; go back to the first question.

3. Why do you want to eat it?

This is a big problem! Do you eat because you want something special? Do you need salt, sugar or carbohydrates? Do you eat because you feel bored, lonely, sad or angry? Do you take fuel before training? It is important to know why to eat because it helps you to identify emotional eating disorders.

Often we eat for reasons other than hunger. Eating is the way we collect, cry and join the community. We will eat to celebrate our birthday. If the child's grades are good, the family will eat ice. When the family died, we stopped for lunch to commemorate the dead. We often do not hear "Let's walk in the garden", but we hear a lot: "Let's meet and have a cup of coffee! Our idea is to come to a place where you can eat just to strengthen your body.

4. How do I feel after eating?

Before you eat, think about what you want after that. Do you feel guilty, angry or bored? Are you swollen? Are You Angry Does This Type of Food Cause Headaches or Abdominal pain? Do you want to keep this food awake all night?

I know that many people keep notes and write everything they eat, but if you write the subject and you're not happy, you'll lose a lot of comparisons. If you see what your food does for you, know if you are sensitive or allergic to food. It can also help you identify triggers that cause you a lot of eating or eating wrong things.

Pro Move: Discuss your doctor to get rid of your diet to understand your food allergies and / or allergies.

Beginner Training: Write notes and record feelings after eating each meal. Look for patterns that make you feel good or bad.

Good luck, these four questions will help you make smarter choices and make you feel comfortable. If you ask yourself these questions, at least before eating, I hope you can slow down and think about what you want to consume. So you can eat consciously or consciously.

Chapter 10

Ways to Soothe Yourself Without Food

After a bad day, are you often at the bottom of the Ben & Jerry peanut butter cup? Although each spoon is sweet and creamy, they eat 1400 calories a day. Emotional diets occur mainly during stressful holidays, but women experience emotional attacks during the year. Susan Albers, Psy.D. Authors of 50 Ways to Relax and Eat, There are 10 ways to deal with stress without calories.

Why Do Women Choose Food Comfortably?

Whether you are old or not, every time you feel pain or experience food reactions because of loneliness, your mother gives you biscuits. An emotional diet is an automatic response for many women. Albers believes that an emotional diet is an instinctive response to repetition. "In other words, we do enough often to know that it can calm down and relax us," she said. "If it looks like you, you will not feel upset." Most women have no other ways to learn to control their emotions. There is no elementary or secondary school that can decide what to do.

The Media is partly responsible for the Emotional Diet:

Albers believes that the link between food and convenience will soon be resolved, especially as the media encourages this mechanism. "Do you often see a woman eating ice cream in a sitcom or drama after a break?" "Look at chocolate and candy, and sell promises of emotional benefits like happiness, love, escape, happiness." This inner tendency gives us a hidden concept of using calories to comfort ourselves naturally and "naturally".

When We Feel Stressed, We Are Ready To Eat:

Before you try to overcome your mother or bother her with food to improve everything, think about the biological response of your body to stress. "The reaction to emotions is a natural and strong response for all of us," Albers said. "We can thank cortically, a stress hormone that causes the need for foods that contain high sugar and fat during stress."

Food is Delicious. What is the Problem?

Right now, you may think that there is nothing more interesting than this, such as a large iceberg roll or a dish of macaroni carbonara, but Albers assures us that food is only a short-term solution. Long-term stress and long-term stress can be a factor in increasing stress. "It seems that food calms down and calms down immediately - if it does not help, you will not do it, right?" But if there is no alternative mechanism for dealing with non-food, emotional food can lead to weight gain. "Some experts say emotional diets exceed 75%, and for many women, the way they deal with emotional food is a big difference.

Benefits of Non-Food Coping Mechanisms:

Easy to get food, it seems to be the easiest (and delicious) way to escape stress, but it is not good for your mood or physical health. Albers recommends learning low-calorie calories to deal with emotions that can significantly improve your health and weight, and allow you to develop long- term, debt-free skills. "This can help you control your emotions and make you feel more confident and happy," Albers said. "To tell the truth, women are under great pressure and need a healthy way to deal with them."

Ways to Soothe Yourself without Food:

Treat Yourself to a Massage:

Have you noticed that you automatically start rubbing your cheeks as the tension increases? Albers says he must move on. "Of course, we do a self-massage and massaging mindfully and mindfully enclosed spaces can release chemicals into your body," she said. "Place a tennis ball under your foot and rub yourself. Or place the ball behind your shoulder blades and stand against the wall. It's a cheap instant massage that can be done on your desk or in the kitchen."

Tag and Cup of Tea:

A study of the Journal of Psychopharmacology, a break with a cup of black tea containing no calories can lower your cortical level by 47%. Albers recommends Republic of Tea chocolate for soft, stress-free fixation.

Sleep a Little:

According to Albers, sleep is crucial to ending an emotional diet. "If you miss even a few hours of sleep, your appetite hormones will be released," says the health expert. "Six to nine hours is optimal." Plan a good night's sleep, as well as appointments and other events.

Chewing Gum:

Keep a pack of sugar-free gum in your bag and use it frequently. It's not only good for your teeth, but it can also help you stop eating emotionally. "A recent study published in the journal Appetite found that chewing gum 15 minutes before eating can significantly reduce appetite and slow down your desire," Albers said. "Brain tests show that your brain is relaxed and awake, so it's good if you want to get bored."

Leave the Desire For You:

Breaking the emotional habit of eating can be the hardest part to finish. Replace your reaction to food if you are stressed by an answer to the training. Instead of taking a candy bar, put on your shoes and go for a walk or do other physical activity that you enjoy. This can be especially helpful if you prefer chocolate or other high-calorie snacks. "A short 20-minute walk, according to a study by the Appetite magazine, can help stop the demand for chocolate," says Albers. Exchanging emotional food with exercise also means increasing your fitness.

Try Chewing Chopsticks:

No, Albers doesn't recommend stealing your pet's green areas, but it encourages people to chew on sticks. "They look like toothpicks, but they are flavors and can be purchased at health food stores or online," she says. "They help people lose weight and quit smoking, they let you chew and chew without calories, and straws can help relieve oral fixation."

Change Your Eating Habits with Goldfish Beads:

Anxiety balls have helped people survive addictive behavior for a long time, so you can no longer get used to eating when they are anxious. "Keep marigold petals in your hand and use them to reduce nervous energy," says Albers, instead of looking for the first stimulus you can find.

Trust in a Deliberate Distraction:

Are you a multitasking person who not only eats emotionally but also sees television, subtitles, speaks on the phone or reads Interest? Albers warns that derived food is a recipe for overeating. But distracting your diet can reduce your desire to eat well. "If you get acquainted with an activity that stimulates your brain but is not too tiring, like just puzzles, knitting and other rhythmic activities, you can calm down and you," she added.

Relax:

"Fear is the center of many of our useless snacks," says Albers. "To calm your body, you can do a simple relaxation exercise: lower your muscles as if you were pop chiffon. Tighten your body and resume position [rag doll] The contrast between tightening and relaxation can help ... solve the fear."

Take a Deep Breath:

Securing your physiological reactions is the key to the collapse of natural cortisol. Imagine blowing through a straw as you breathe out. Count to 10 for slow and deep inhalation. If you lower your breathing, your body will think it goes to bed. That way, only the rest of your body is reported

Although the emotional diet is a "natural response", Albers does not believe that diet is the only way to control cortical levels. Suggested soothing activities such as relaxing, sleeping, drinking tea and other non-food activities to restore the balance of cortical level. "I like the classic logo," Calgon says. "It's a rare and successful example of advertising that provides women with another healthy way to overcome stress."

List of Tasks to be processed:

Traditionally, the task list includes such elements as bill payment and dry cleaning. Consider creating another column of personal activities you'll always use. Write this investment in your mental health, for example. Sleep more or eat more fruits. Studies have shown that if you just type this, you will do something first. (Watch this video to learn how to discuss these tips.)

Get more vitamin D:

Vitamin D is closely related to mood and is usually low in winter and rainy days. To improve your mood, consider checking your doctor for vitamin D levels. You can also eat more foods rich in vitamin D, such as eggs, mushrooms and milk.

Get Some Green Food:

In Japan, forest therapy refers to your mental health. Studies have shown that the country has only 15 minutes to help lower blood pressure and improve mood.

Stop Dieting:

People often tend to prepare for a spring break, summer vacation and holidays. Instead, try to focus on food, not on cutting food, but to pay more attention to your eating habits. If they do not eat in front of their mobile phones, people will be happier, eat less, and enjoy food, a recent study shows.

Stand Up:

Standing position contributes to blood circulation and public health. A five-minute rest during the meeting could reduce blood sugar by 34% and increase life expectancy by two years, according to a study by the American Diabetes Association. Try to remind you to be on time by setting the alarm on your phone.

Be Nice to Yourself:

My motto is: do not look back; you do not. Pay attention to what to expect. We can do this by ignoring the past. You can also give you "adult time" every day and spend five minutes to meet and breathe.

Tackle Negative Soothing Habits Tied to Food:

Dealing with your feelings in this blog means negative eating habits, in reference to some emotional states. Depending on your progress, this may mean that you are constantly screaming in an unmindful state, refusing food or feeling helpless without feeling like you own or leave your body. If you are not an emotional person but you have negative emotional comfort, you may get something out of this news. This is about how to develop a quiet model - and a tool to answer this question objectively.

Part 1: What?

What is an emotional diet? Negative habits related to the emotional state. If you eat too much or eat too much or lose control, this medication may be.

You can eat in front of the TV for a long time. It is an unmindful food, the operation of a machine produces a chemical state in the brain. You can stop the food then swing the other and desire. Or live a state of constant control and pain - unable to escape and enjoy the food, always afraid.

When you eat emotionally, it comes from a place where stress and emotional pain are dealt with. Stimulates the lack of connection with the body and its need: Food is not linked to food and nutrition, so it is a big problem. We cannot create a system in the context of taking care of ourselves, fear and abuse will be another matter. It is very important that it is related to the emotional process and has nothing to do with the actual food. The actual nature of the food is not related to this problem - except how you change your body after years of being abused by your body. The first inspiration for an emotional diet has nothing to do with your love of diet. This is the position in which the things that you do hang out. If you grow up elsewhere, you may become a bet on assets. Why should I emphasize this? Because if you encounter this problem, you can keep your physical image - you can find something like "food habits" on Google, which means you cannot choose the right food balance. No - this is a game for kids. You can read thousands of health magazines about good nutrition. It is impossible to understand the circumstances. Alienation leads to a lack of physical trust for our body and us. You cannot see the compass, so you are afraid of nodding. So the driver's imbalance - just like driving with lead feet. "I'm hungry!" I cannot control it! "

Food is a metaphor for how we deal with anxiety and pain. We run or win or hide or accept or fall apart. We do the same for food. In Buddhism, they refer to this kind of mentality as a kind of taking/fear, type of rejection/anger or type of rejection/amnesty. Depending on your type, you respond in a predictable manner, indicating that you are used to dealing with bad habits.

It has many important aspects of our hearts. Eat and Live. If you give them something, give him life and food. You can also remove the blank by filling it. In chemistry, your body also receives natural painkillers rich in calories and fat. For this reason, food is mixed with issues of dignity, emptiness and desire - it metaphorically connects love that nourishes and accepts emotions. This makes it an easy target for self-insurance.

If the entry barrier is too weak, it is easy to accept negative habits. Unlike drugs, eating is a part of life. Continue to force yourself. This is the basic goal of society: obesity, beauty and nutrition everywhere. The evolution of these problems is linked to the lack of self-commitment and the true value of food. But nothing to do with the food!! Their problems are related to pain management. As with any other bad habit, training is required to break it.

Part 2: Why

All food problems are associated with low self-esteem. This is not to save you but to yourself. Be punished! "Stand by yourself!" A way to focus on what you can control. "My body is a problem in my life." The result is that you play puppet shows and do not really face the source of fear in your room. All eating disorders are a way to control the source of pain by doing what you can see. They call it external (thinking) to reduce overwhelming pressure. Otherwise, it will only make you feel nervous and scared. There is no way to get rid of fear! If you do not use drugs, do not drink or cut yourself, so if you cannot talk about your pain or understand it as an adult, you will keep it and open food. Eating disorders are associated with discomfort and inevitable trauma

- they are particularly common in families with low moods or feelings of pain such as anxiety and weakness. If you are a victim, you may be familiar with the dynamics of your family.

So this is something very old. It has nothing to do with the amount of food you love. This may be your reason, but this is a mistake. The characteristic of this cycle is that the chemicals disappear and become hungry, desperate, unbalanced, and tired and look. It looks like you are helping to take medication by breaking your identity and investing resources.

•When you eat your pain: you curse. This is the dynamic bottom. It will never be filled with desire and emptiness, but it requires a lot of effort. You do not speak, become invisible. It was originally a chemical way of complacency, but it also led to the expected result: If you are fat, you will still be invisible. This is also associated unmindfully with the abandonment of sexual interest. When you are very skinny, people will continue to move forward and feel uncomfortable.

•If you control your suffering: you are speaking the truth. Often it is a binger/burger. If we control our family or "small adults," we control our feelings and inability to control eating. This is a guy A, rebel, you fucking on the table, a little family member. You stumbled in your pain: filling up and stabbing the true feelings of their careers. This is a distraction and will be a new job. If you do not want to be aware of fear, you will. You give him the key and say, "Go now."

•If you force others to take care of your pain and loss of strength, you are the child. Often the loss of appetite/encounter. Lack of food is a means of ensuring comfort through continued occupation, concentration and disability. This means that you can completely remove the experiment and become an object of your body. This is usually shared by parents and his expectations are unrealistic. In fact, this is a way for parents to love and care for you, just as if you were going back to childhood. This disease replaces all that can cause pain. It's more than just a glass figure - your vision is always distorted. This is a way to completely remove your senses from your body and become an object controlled by a third-party cooling system. This is the most dangerous separation between body and mind because it affects your vision. Your chemical disability is most common because your mind is affected by undernourishment.

In all these patterns, there is a separation that leads to serious malfunction, so that it replaces all innate knowledge. So you always interact and interact with this imbalance without knowing what to do, but calm down and remain dominant - and for any addiction, this is a balanced action. Full-time review work. What is the unmindful thing we always wanted: playing a game gives us a reason to feel pain.

Until you decide to reconnect with your innate balance through this reactive state. The solution is to go back to your body and listen to it again. I know it's pretty scary: a house where you grewup is probably scary and dangerous. But - the balance is yours. It takes time, courage and dedication - but you get there. You need to rebuild the walls, hang the wallpaper. And then it becomes more beautiful and clearer than ever.

So let's go to the tools!

Part 3: How to Tool

It is probably a battle that you fought hard. So I think hope and understanding is the first answer. Although you have tried to find help for yourself, an important part of this puzzle is to determine the underlying feelings underlying this reality - in therapy and most importantly - the commitment to achieving the right one. It must be necessary. You only have to determine your health and well-being. It cannot be conditional on maintaining a certain weight - it must be pure effort. I will be free from this suffering and be happy. And I do what it takes. And I tell you that this goal leads to everything you want. It all begins with the goal of loving and knowing each other.

In addition, exercise for chemical support is very useful. * Unless you exercise - I want to say breathing exercises are important to you - sitting in a meditation position. And depending on how long it took, I recommend consulting a nutrition expert with a background in ED, or better yet, a discovery route for nature - someone who can help you find the right supplements and the right amount of food you need for have. Your needs are based on your personal history. In other words, create a lot of structure for yourself! Defeat it with all the intelligence you have. The safer you feel, the easier it is to trust that road. Create a personal team of experts.

TOOLS 1. E-CARD LIST

You have done this thing now and you will find all sorts of tools and move away from it. To do this, you must become objective. Imagine suppressing growth. Go to different places and remove them. Once you find your way through the chemical claws involved in your emotions, magic will be broken forever!

It starts with making the right emergency list or "wireless list" in our case, and so I mean a list of 10 things you can do as soon as you feel in a dangerous zone. This list = what can you do to calm down? For example, I have everything from going to podcasts, podium sites in my office and Alanon meetings on my list of wiring sets. It's about making sure you're insured in every situation! And calm. The point is to reassure yourself beyond what you feel until it becomes a natural habit and you can see the positive results. Don't take it easy. Treat him like the devil, waiting with a listening ear at the door.

If you feel worried, go to your list. If you think you're worried this weekend, fill out this label with items from your list. You publish back-ups on back-ups on your agenda. These are huge amounts of structure and support. Know your safe areas and go before you start whispering your grief.

2. RED WARNING: SEND A WARNING

Something like "Bottomless Pit" You need a mantra or slogan that you can call if you notice that things are going in the wrong way. It's about an increased awareness of the voice, which is currently very quiet. Stay intimate in mindfulness. Ed's voice is different from yours. She looks like a creepy person and is probably encouraged by certain environments and situations where certain emotional dynamics arise. Their job is to become aware of what they are - and to prepare.

For example, if you have a family and everything is hidden under the surface, this attitude will excite you - even if you are working. Discover the rituals, triggers and exercise to call them. "I do not think there is no minimum." You can feel her arrival - very sensitive to them and fucking there. Allow yourself to choose rationally if you cannot deal with it, do not go! If you can, please share a partner in your event. Tell them the word code. Ask for help make sure they will marry you there! You have an alternate partner to connect to.

This is the time of purchase to pass the trigger. The more you fall the closer you get to safety. Give yourself time to find the item in the list of electronic fonts.

3. **Change Addicts:**

You will likely choose this habit in a mindful state. Maybe because you think you have no choice. You will always do this. This is not the case. This is a comfort addiction. But you might hate it. You may be tired of it already and hope you are not part of you. You envy others. This habit is as addictive as most habits. But not you, you do not like it, your body does not feel good. This is not what you really want. This is a kind of coercion.

So start from there: disconnect it from you, that person.

All you have to do is focus on the moment before you start - and find an alternative addiction. This is not forever - just grab some power from the current addiction. If you can go shopping online instead of shopping - try the size. Let's talk about nutrition now because it seems to be the least healthy. You get a dietitian, buy a set of books, and then start a new chapter of meditation, when you are depressed and participate in a new class of yoga, you will have a new friend and you will try to get out all these things. This is something you can put a lot of energy and attention to.

The goal is - the moment you think you will enter the cycle of addiction, when you are concerned, you will use something new. As I said before, everything about creating a new connection has nothing to do with food. It takes only a few minutes to succeed - let yourself go in a completely different direction from food.

If you are in doubt, please leave home! Get out of the door and leave you anywhere and go. Do something different so you cannot do it anymore. For me, this is yoga, then walking, then contact a friend, and then go somewhere while listening to the podcast, even the dark outside, my dog refuses to walk. You can and will develop a new habit, and your body will have a similar dependence on it - but you should put yourself into action, although your mind can reach the upper hand at first. Do your best to do what you can. You will feel wrong or will be sustainable, and then you will find within a few weeks that they are already valid.

4. Clean House

Otherwise - proof of the environment. This means taking snacks from your home, eating lunches in advance, skipping happy hours after work, trimming all models from Instagram Recipe - no matter what makes you worried and dirty - you should go!

All this is not forever - so you can restore balance! Will be back. It takes to reset everything a year or so - the hardest part is choosing the exit.

Finally...

I know that when you feel helpless and have tried everything and lost hope, that's very bad. When you go there, I can say that once you are not afraid of this road and start walking for your health - things become clearer than you are now. You've created the right support and will never be alone. You all have different strengths, not just your own strength. If you write, you may suffer alone - you think I am intelligent, I can always do more than others, if I cannot help me - no one can do it. Why not? Your life is based on a model.

Well, this is the fakest we are confused. Start looking for support now. Hire them. Think of it as a ball you want to win, and do it right. Not a person. Just fucking to end it if you are somewhere now, assuming you are different and want to know if you can stop fighting, and the answer is if you continue to search for your choice and ban it - stop hiding and point to it. You will definitely solve it and solve this problem literally. It is a promise that never loses hope. So this takes the rest of your life.

CPSIA information can be obtained
at www.ICGtesting.com
Printed in the USA
BVHW041505030621
608739BV00002B/210

9 781801 325318